ACCORDING TO THE SCRIPTURES

ACCORDING TO THE SCRIPTURES

THE SUB-STRUCTURE OF NEW TESTAMENT THEOLOGY

By

C. H. DODD

PROFESSOR EMERITUS IN
THE UNIVERSITY OF CAMBRIDGE

LONDON: NISBET & CO., LTD.
22 BERNERS STREET, W.1

First published in November 1952
Reprinted . . . . March 1953

Made and Printed in Great Britain

VIRO   REVERENDO

IOHANNI   ALEXANDRO   MACKAY

SEMINARII SACRAE THEOLOGIAE

IN OPPIDO PRINCIPIS NOVOCAESARIENSI

PRAESIDI

CVM VIRIS DOCTISSIMIS

EIVSDEM SEMINARII

PROFESSORIBVS DOCTORIBVS MAGISTRIS

HOSPITIBVS   HOSPES

D.   D.

AVCTOR

PREFACE

THIS book represents a course of Stone Lectures delivered at Princeton Theological Seminary, New Jersey, in March, 1950. The text has been revised and in large part re-written.

C. H. D.

CAMBRIDGE.
February, 1952.

CONTENTS

ACCORDING TO THE SCRIPTURES

I

THE PROBLEM

THE historical study of New Testament theology, as distinct from dogmatic or systematic theology, is faced by the difficult task of discovering the true starting-point of the development which the New Testament writings exhibit. It seems that the soundest method towards that end is to isolate, among the rich variety of these writings, those elements which are so widely common to them that they must be regarded as forming part of a central tradition, by which they were all more or less controlled. It should then be possible to arrive at some probable estimate of the extent to which this common tradition is primitive, or at least capable of being traced back to as early a period in the history of the Church as our research can reasonably expect to reach. This would give us, not necessarily, or not only, a theoretical basis for doctrine, but a genuinely chronological starting point for the history of Christian thought.

It may fairly be said that a considerable degree of consent has now been achieved about the character and contents of the common and central tradition. It appears to have at its core what the New Testament itself calls the *kerygma*, or proclamation of the Gospel. In its most summary form the *kerygma* consists of the announcement of certain historical events in a setting which displays the significance of those events. The events in question are those of the appearance of Jesus in history—His ministry, sufferings and death and His subsequent manifestation of Himself to His followers as risen from the dead and invested with the glory of another world—and the emergence of the Church as a society distinguished by the power and activity of the Holy Spirit, and looking forward to the return of its Lord as Judge and Saviour of the world.

The significance attached to these events is mainly indicated by references to the Old Testament. In the few clauses of the *kerygma* which are preserved in I Cor. xv. 3-5 it is said that Christ died, and rose the third day, "according to the scriptures." In the more formal summary outlines of the *kerygma* which are given in Acts it is a constant theme that in the coming of Christ, His death and resurrection, the prophecies are fulfilled.[1]

Such, in very broad terms, is the core of the common and central tradition. By comparison of *data* in the Acts and in the Pauline epistles it can be traced back to a very early stage indeed, and may fairly be called primitive. The more closely we study the writings of the New Testament, the more clear it becomes that in most of them, at any rate, this apostolic *kerygma* is a basic standard of reference for everything that is set forth as part of the Christian Gospel. It is itself, properly speaking, pre-theological, and does not bring us very far on the road to that reflective and reasoned presentation of the truth of the Gospel which is Christian theology. But it underlies everything. It may be described as the ground-plan of New Testament theology.

In various parts of the New Testament, notably in the

[1] I assume here the results of the argument set forth in my book, *The Apostolic Preaching and its Developments* (Hodder & Stoughton, 1936).

epistles of Paul, the Epistle to the Hebrews, and the Gospel and Epistles of John, we have a theological edifice constructed upon this plan. The style of building differs considerably. The theology of Paul, of John, and of the author to the Hebrews, though based upon a common tradition of the centre, is far from uniform. As church architecture, based upon a universal general plan, may show the various characteristics of Romanesque, Gothic or Baroque, so each of these theologians builds after his own style. It is a great merit of modern critical study of the New Testament that it has made us appreciate the individuality of the great theologians of the apostolic age, and the rich diversity of their teaching. The question now before us is this: Granted that each of these early thinkers followed the general tradition embodied in the apostolic *kerygma*, and faithfully conserved its main outline, have they anything in common beyond the bare outline? To put it otherwise, given the ground-plan, and the majestic buildings erected to its pattern, can we find a substructure —a part of the actual edifice—which is common to them all, or are the several buildings individually different from the foundation up?

In describing the contents of the *kerygma*, I have distinguished the *events* which it announces, on the one hand, and on the other hand the *significance* which it attaches to them. We shall normally seek the starting point for theology in those parts of the *kerygma* which suggest significance. As I have remarked, this significance is indicated mainly by reference to the prophecies of the Old Testament. The programmatic discourse attributed to Peter on the Day of Pentecost in Acts ii begins (after the rhetorical exordium) with the pronouncement, "This is that which was spoken by the prophet," (ii. 16) and it is punctuated by citations from the Old Testament all through. Similarly, in the discourse of Peter and John before the Sanhedrin in chapter iii, we are told, "the things which God foreshowed by the mouth of all the prophets, . . . he thus fulfilled" (iii. 18). In the type of *kerygma* attributed to Paul in Acts xiii we read "We bring you good tidings of the promise made to the fathers, how that God fulfilled the same to our children" (xiii. 32-33). The "good tidings" consist primarily in the news of what has happened; to understand *how* they are "good tidings," they must be related to what has gone before. How vital this reference to Scripture is, appears from another clause in Peter's Pentecostal discourse. In his brief report of the facts, he comes to the point that Jesus was handed over by the Jews to the Romans, who put Him to death. The inclusion of so tragic a report in a proclamation which purports to be "good tidings" needs some justification. Peter offers the key to such justification by adding that all this took place "by the determinate counsel and foreknowledge of God" (Acts ii. 23). Such a bald and provocative statement as that cannot have been intended to stand by itself. It was incumbent upon the preacher, having said so much, to establish what was the determinate counsel of God. The only way in which this could be discovered (for anyone who accepted the fundamental postulates of biblical religion) was by consulting the record of God's dealings with His people in Scripture; for no devout and believing Jew would suppose that the human mind could by speculative reasoning discover the counsel of the Most High. Thus the Church was committed, by the very terms of its *kerygma*, to a formidable task of biblical research, primarily for the purpose of clarifying its own understanding of the momentous events out of which it had emerged, and also for the purpose of making its Gospel intelligible to the outside public.

According to the Acts of the Apostles this task was essayed from the very beginning of the Church's existence as an organized and active body. There are numerous places where the methods employed by early Christian preachers are instructively depicted.

In Acts viii. 26-38, for example, we have an account, given with the vividness characteristic of Lucan narrative, of an encounter between the evangelist Philip and an Ethiopian visitor to Jerusalem—the first recorded approach of a Christian preacher to a person neither Jew by birth nor resident in Palestine. The Ethiopian, having made the pilgrimage to Jerusalem, has acquired a scroll of the Book of Isaiah, and is whiling away the tedium of a long drive by reading it—reading it aloud of course, after the manner of the time. The narrator has thus skilfully prepared for the introduction of a passage from the fifty-third chapter of Isaiah which, in his belief (and as we shall see, in the general belief of the primitive Church), declared in unmistakable terms "the determinate counsel of God"; and he goes on to tell how the evangelist forthwith showed this to be "fulfilled" in the Gospel facts.

Again, in Acts xviii. 24-28, we have a brief and not too perspicuous account of the work of Apollos. This rather enigmatic personage is described as a man of learning (or perhaps an eloquent man, ἀνὴρ λόγιος) and an outstanding biblical scholar, hailing from the great university city of Alexandria. He appeared at Ephesus as a disciple of John the Baptist and began teaching, quite accurately (says the author), "the things concerning Jesus." How much Luke intended to include under that head is not clear, but he evidently felt that it fell short of the full Christian Gospel. Apollos however was taken in hand by Priscilla and Aquila, who expounded to him "the way of God" more accurately. They were then satisfied to recommend him as a teacher to the young Church at Corinth, and there he formed close ties with its members, and held public sessions in which he set about convincing (the imperfect διακατηλέγχετο) the Jews, by demonstrating through passages from the scriptures that the Messiah of whom they spoke was no other than Jesus (εἶναι τὸν χριστὸν Ἰησοῦν). We could wish that our author had been more explicit; but we seem safe in concluding that according to his view the Christian Gospel could not be adequately or convincingly set forth unless the communication of facts about Jesus (τὰ περὶ τοῦ Ἰησοῦ) was supported by references to the Old Testament which gave significance to the facts, and that it was a prime concern of Christian missionaries to provide and interpret such references.

The same method, fundamentally, is attributed to Paul. At Thessalonica, for example (Acts xvii. 2-3), he followed what is expressly said to have been his general practice, of commending the Gospel by arguing from the Scriptures. He "opened up" the meaning of certain passages from the Old Testament, and "adduced" them as evidence for his conclusions (διελέξατο αὐτοῖς ἀπὸ τῶν γραφῶν, διανοίγων καὶ παρατιθέμενος). The points that he made are summed up as follows: (i) that the Messiah is a suffering Messiah; (ii) that the Messiah rises from the dead; and (iii) that this Messiah is identical with Jesus.

Again, in Acts xxvi we have an account of a speech which Paul is said to have delivered in the presence of Agrippa II, and in which he briefly states and defends his missionary work. No good Jew, he contends, ought to take exception to his preaching, since there is nothing in it which cannot be justified out of "Moses and the prophets." In particular, the three points to which exception was taken are all attested by scripture, viz. (i) that the Messiah is a suffering Messiah; (ii) that the

Messiah is to rise from the dead, and (iii) that He is to proclaim the light of salvation both to Israel and to the Gentiles (Acts xxvi. 22-23). Two of the points, we observe, are repeated from the other passage we noted: the third point is new. Paul does not here mention the point that the Messiah is to be identified with Jesus, while he adds the point that the Gospel is for Gentiles as well as for Jews. But the general similarity of the two schemes is striking.

It is particularly interesting to note the form in which the main heads of Paul's discussions are stated. They are introduced by the particle εἰ used interrogatively: "*whether* the Messiah is a suffering Messiah. . . ." This interrogative form is eminently appropriate to a method of teaching which is described by the verb διαλέγεσθαι, "to discuss." We conclude that in addition to what is called "preaching" (κηρύσσειν), early Christian missionaries also employed the method of discussion, in which certain questions were propounded—questions arising unavoidably out of the *kerygma*—and answers sought by a study of the Old Testament.

Luke evidently believed that the three great questions which he has formulated were in no way peculiar to Paul; for so much at least we may infer from the close of his Gospel, where he has appended to an account of the appearance of the risen Christ to His disciples a summary of what they learned from Him after His resurrection: "it is written (a) that the Messiah is to suffer and (b) to rise from the dead the third day, and (c) that in His name repentance leading to forgiveness of sins is to be proclaimed to all nations": once again the three headings of Paul's argument before Agrippa (xxiv. 46-47).

The Lucan writings are in the first place evidence for missionary practice at the date of their composition. So far however as Paul is concerned we are in a position to test Luke's statements by the direct testimony of the Apostle's own writings. We have indeed nowhere in the Pauline epistles a full discussion of the questions propounded regarding the scriptural warrant for the Messiahship of Jesus, or for His sufferings and resurrection. None of the epistles was written to people who needed convincing on those points. It was enough simply to set down the fact that all this was "according to the scriptures." But the last head, "whether He is to proclaim the light both to Israel and to the Gentiles" ("first to the Jew; then to the Greek," as Paul formulated it briefly, Rom. i. 16) happened to be a matter on which there was still not complete agreement among Christians, and we have a full-length discussion of it in Romans ix-xi, which provides a striking example of Paul's method as described in Acts xvii. 2-3. The terms "opening up" and "adducing" are apt.

The method is to take certain passages of Scripture, to examine them in relation to a broad context, and to determine their meaning and application to the existing situation by comparison with other passages from Scripture. In the course of the discussion the apostle quotes from the following books of the Old Testament: Genesis, Exodus, Leviticus, Numbers, Deuteronomy, Samuel, Kings, Job, Psalms, Isaiah, Jeremiah, Hosea, Joel, Malachi. This is evidence of the thorough and extensive biblical research which lies behind Paul's exposition of the Gospel. It should be added that the argument, complex and compressed as it is, proceeds by strict sequence from step to step, and is, with one or two possible exceptions, completely cogent, granted the pre-suppositions common to Paul and to those whom he addressed. The qualification indeed is itself scarcely necessary; if one takes the pains to understand exactly what is implied in the various steps in the argument, there is very little which does not contribute to a strictly logical presentation of his case from first principles. A careful study of it, for which this is not the place, opens up a genuinely historical understanding of the Gospel facts in relation to their antecedents in the history of Israel. This however would be a study of the mind of Paul, a single and towering genius, and we are in search rather of that which was common to the general mind of the Church.

Let us, then, take a further example from a different author, the unknown scholar and theologian to whom we owe the Epistle to the Hebrews. This epistle is in large part a prolonged exposition of portions of the Old Testament with reference to the Christian Gospel. But take one brief passage, ii. 5-13. Here the question at issue is, to put it broadly, the status and dignity of Jesus Christ; that is to say, it might be placed under the Lucan heading "that the Messiah is Jesus." The author begins by citing at full length a passage from Psalm viii: "What is man that thou art mindful of him, or the son of man that thou visitest him? Thou didst for a short time make him inferior to angels: thou hast crowned him with glory and honour; thou hast put all things under his feet" (4-6). The writer observes that the last clause here is to be taken strictly: "all things" means the entire universe, without exception. It is therefore clear that the terms "man" and "son of man" cannot refer to the human race as we know it, for man is not yet lord of creation. On the other hand we have seen Jesus (in the terms of the Psalm) first brought low for a time, and then "crowned with glory and honour," and that, by virtue of His passion and death.[1] Hence we

[1] That all things are subjected to Him the author has already shown from Ps. cx. 1: "Sit thou at my right hand till I make thy enemies the footstool of thy feet" (Heb. i. 13).

must conclude that the "Son of Man" of the Psalm is Jesus as Christ. But that implies that the glory with which He is crowned is intended to be shared with the whole human race, for the Psalm speaks of "man": in Him God designs to bring *many* sons to glory. This is what is referred to in Ps. xxii. 22, "I will proclaim thy name among my brothers; in the midst of the church I will sing thy praise," as well as in Is. viii. 18, "Behold! I and the children whom God has given me." The conclusion is that Jesus is Messiah, or Son of Man, in the sense that He has passed through death to glory and universal sovereignty as representative Head of a redeemed mankind.

As a further example of method we may take another passage from the same epistle, Heb. iii. 7 - iv. 9. The question at issue here is not precisely one of those listed by Luke, but it is one which bears upon the fundamental assumption of the *kerygma*, that the eschatological hope is now realized. The author takes the word "rest" (κατάπαυσις) as the key to the blessings of the new era. He cites at length a passage from Ps. xcv, which ends, "unto whom I swore in my wrath: They shall not enter into my rest." Who, he asks, are these persons who are not to enter into God's rest? Those who were faithless and disobedient. It follows that those who are to enter into the rest are, by contrast, the faithful (οἱ πιστεύσαντες, which for him and his readers connotes "Christian believers"). But what is the "rest" spoken of? It might be supposed to mean that Israelites who in the wilderness were faithful while others were unfaithful would end their wanderings in the land of promise. But this is impossible, because the Psalm, written by David centuries after the time of Joshua, by implication offers entrance into rest "to-day." It is God's own rest, or Sabbath, that is meant: see Gen. ii. 2: "On that day God rested from all His works."

That is what is here meant by "*my* rest": there is a "sabbath", a day of rest, still in store for the people of God. Conclusion: "To-day" has come: let us hasten to enter into God's rest.

Paul, and the author to the Hebrews, were trained scholars, and both were men of great and original individuality. It would be precarious to infer that precisely these methods of scripture interpretation were employed by the common run of Christian teachers. Let us look at a much more "popular" work, the First Epistle of Peter. In the passage i. 22 - ii. 10 the author is dealing with the theme of the new people of God—the people "born again" through the word of the living God. Here he seems to be going outside the scriptural basis of Christian preaching, for "rebirth" is not a biblical idea. But the reference to the Word of God brings him back to bed-rock. He quotes from Is. xl. 6-8, a passage which ends with the clause "the Word of the Lord endures for ever"; and he adds: "this is the word of the Gospel preached to you." In receiving it (he proceeds), Christians have (in the words of Ps. xxxiv. 8) "tasted how gracious the Lord is." The Lord, he continues (meaning, of course, our Lord Jesus Christ), is the stone spoken of in Ps. cxviii. 22, rejected by men, but made by God both corner stone, and also, as Is. xxviii. 16 has it, the foundation stone of Zion. But the same stone, as Isaiah says in viii. 14, is to the faithless and the disobedient "a stone of stumbling and a rock of offence." No wonder, then, that Christ is rejected by many. But those who accept Him are themselves "living stones" built upon Him as foundation, and are consequently, as sundry passages of the Old Testament declare God's people to be, a royal priesthood, a holy nation, a people for God's own possession, whose priestly function it is, to announce His mighty acts. In short, what Hosea said has come true: they who were once called Lo-ammi, "not my people," are now called Ammi, "my people."

We observe that, unlike Paul and the author to the Hebrews, the writer of this passage is not arguing. He is setting forth the character of the Church's life, founded upon Christ as He is made known in the Gospel, by recalling passages from the Old Testament which recite the attributes of the people of God, which passages are *assumed* by him and his readers to be applicable to Christ and His Church. It is clear that the writer can confidently assume this application, without argument; from which we may fairly infer that an already accepted tradition of scriptural interpretation lies behind this epistle.

But now, if we turn back to Paul and the author to the Hebrews, we discover that they too make certain assumptions without which their carefully sustained arguments would not stand. Take the latter first. In chs. iii-iv, on the "rest" of God's people, the author is clearly arguing to show that a psalm not hitherto related specifically to the themes of the Gospel has a real bearing on them. But in ch. ii, on Jesus as Son of Man, the case is different. He assumes without argument that the one-hundred-and-tenth psalm refers to Christ, and uses its opening words (by implication) to support his reference to Christ of the words "thou hast put all things under his feet" from Ps. viii. 6.[1] Again, he assumes without argument that the passages from which he cites "I will proclaim thy name among my brothers," and "I and the children whom God has given me," refer to Christ. Here again we seem to discern a common tradition lying behind the original contribution of a single learned author, a tradition which

---

[1] He appears to find it necessary to argue for the application of Ps. viii to Christ; yet we shall see reason to suppose that this psalm too had already been so applied (pp. 32-34).

he shared with those to whom he wrote. Similarly, although
Paul in the main tries to start from an understanding of
the biblical text just as it stands in its context, yet his
selection of passages seems to be largely dictated by the
postulate that certain particular parts of scripture have
direct relevance to the events announced in the *kerygma*.
Thus, he *argues* that the passage from Deut. xxx. 12-13,
about the word in the mouth and in the heart, has reference to the "word of Christ," or the Gospel (Rom. x. 6-10);
but he appears to *assume* rather than to argue that the
passage from Hosea about Ammi and Lo-ammi, and the
passages from Isaiah about the Remnant, about the
Foundation stone of Zion, and about the Stone of stumbling, belong to a group of prophecies which directly
illuminate the situation brought about by the coming of
Christ. And these passages, with one exception, are those
which we have seen to be adduced under the same assumption by the author of I Peter.

The impression, therefore, that we derive from examination of such applications of Old Testament Scripture to
the events of the *kerygma* by the New Testament theologians is that they are working upon certain accepted
assumptions, and that they have behind them a good deal
of fundamental work upon the subject which must have
gone on in very early days. This impression must be
tested by closer inspection of the *data*.

It was suggested long ago that the phenomena of
scriptural quotation in the New Testament might be
accounted for by the hypothesis that a collection of
"messianic proof-texts" was compiled at a very early
date, and that this was used by New Testament writers.
The hypothesis was worked out most elaborately by
Rendel Harris, first in a series of articles, which were
subsequently published, with additional matter, in two

slim volumes entitled *"Testimonies"* (1916, 1920). Harris's argument started from two ends. First, we have a volume under the name of Cyprian entitled *Testimonia*, containing just such a collection, organized and classified for the use of Christian apologists. It is easy to see that Cyprian is little more than an editor who revised and enlarged an earlier work. Harris showed abundantly how substantial portions of the classified collection can be recognized in such earlier writers as Tertullian, Irenaeus and Justin. At the other end, we have the New Testament itself, where Harris noted certain points: in particular (*a*) certain passages tend to be quoted by more than one writer; (*b*) when they are so quoted, the said writers not infrequently agree in a reading different from that of the LXX, as if they were using in common a different translation, though such translation can seldom be identified, except in so far as some of these peculiar renderings reappear in the later versions of Aquila or Theodotion; (*c*) certain passages tend to appear in combination in more than one New Testament book, suggesting that two or more authors took them from a source in which they were already combined; and this suggestion is all the stronger where it appears that a writer has inadvertently attributed two passages from different authors to the same author, as for example Mark (i. 2-3) gives a composite citation from Malachi and Isaiah and attributes the whole to Isaiah, an error which might easily arise if he were drawing the quotations not from copies of the books in question, but from an anthology which gave the two prophecies together; (*d*) groups of passages tend to recur, connected by some key word or idea, e.g. various passages which speak of a stone—the stone which the builders rejected, the corner-stone of Zion, the stone of stumbling, and Daniel's stone cut without hands, which overthrew the great image and ground it to powder. Such groupings seem to anticipate the classification of testimonies in Cyprian and others, where we find, e.g. the passages just referred to under the catch heading *"Quod idem* (Jesus) *Lapis dictus sit."*

Harris drew the conclusion that the original Book of Testimonies was, if not the earliest literary product of the Church, at least one of the earliest, antedating every canonical writing, and that its compiler was Matthew the Apostle; and he adopted from F. C. Burkitt the suggestion that it was this compilation which Papias meant when he said that "Matthew composed the Logia." The subsequent fortunes of this most important book he was able, with his immense and curious learning, to trace through innumerable writings, in various languages, of the patristic period, showing that it was used, re-edited and enlarged constantly throughout this period; and he even ventured to identify a sixteenth century MS. preserved on Mount Athos, containing a work against the Jews in five books which consists mainly of a collection of Testimonies, and is attributed to "Matthew the Monk," as a late form of the primitive Testimony-book, with the name of its true author confusedly preserved. This final stage of the argument, I fancy, no one, perhaps not even Harris himself,[1] took very seriously. But the main theory commanded wide attention and gained the assent of many scholars. In fact it may be said that in Great Britain at least Rendel Harris's book was the starting point of modern study of the use of the Old Testament in the New. It has, I believe, been assumed by most recent British writers that some such anthology of quotations was actually in existence at an early period, and that its use by New Testament

[1] I have heard him whimsically parody his own methods with an apparent seriousness which imposed upon some of his hearers.

writers is the best explanation of the phenomena before us.

For myself, I worked with Harris's hypothesis for many years. Many of the observations which I have already made, and shall make, I owe originally to the study of his work. But I have come to think that his theory outruns the evidence, which is not sufficient to prove so formidable a literary enterprise at so early a date. Indeed, if such a work existed, was known to be the work of an apostle, and was held in such high esteem that Paul, the author to the Hebrews, the evangelists, the author of Acts, and one after another of the early patristic writers made it their *vade mecum*, it is scarcely to be understood that it should have been omitted from the Canon, should never be referred to, unless in Papias's enigmatic note, and should not have emerged into the light of day, as a substantive work, until Cyprian edited it in the middle of the third century. Further, while the examples which Harris gave under the four heads I have mentioned are striking enough, it is difficult to extend the list of such examples under the heads (b), (c) and (d). The cases (b) where two or more writers agree in non-septuagintal readings are not numerous, certainly not more numerous than cases where one agrees with the LXX and the other differs, or where both differ from the LXX and from one another. The list under (c) where identical combinations of passages occur in more than one writer, is a comparatively short one, and while these cases need to be accounted for, they may be quite special and exceptional cases, insufficient to prove a general theory. Finally, the recurrence of the group of passages in which a "stone" is used as a symbol, corresponding as it does to an established grouping in known testimony books, is indeed striking, but is almost the only one of its kind—the only one certainly which carries any particular weight. In my judgment, the evidence points in a somewhat different direction, as I shall try to show.

The attempt to discover just how the Old Testament was employed to elucidate the *kerygma* in the earliest period accessible to us and in circles which exerted permanent influence on Christian thought, is one which we are bound to make in seeking the substructure of New Testament theology; because, if we can discover it, we shall be on the way to understanding the concept of "fulfilment," which appears to govern the early Christian interpretation of the Gospel events as proclaimed in the *kerygma*.

II

TESTIMONIES

SINCE the revival of interest in the Old Testament among New Testament scholars—a most salutary revival—we have had many learned essays upon the old theme, "Novum testamentum in vetere latet, vetus in novo patet"; but some of them, I think have not altogether avoided the dangerous ground of speculation and fancy, where associations of ideas arising in the critic's own mind have been treated as evidence for original connections. We need a study which shall be based upon verifiable evidence that *this* New Testament writer did in fact refer his readers to *that* passage of the Old Testament in connection with this or that particular theme of the Gospel or of Christian theology. Such evidence is available, if not perhaps on the scale or in the quantity we might have wished. Upon that basis, and by comparison of one passage with others, and of one writer with another, we may be able to draw inferences regarding the general principles which underlie the use of *testimonia* by these writers, and perhaps to advance to further inferences regarding the employment of the Old Testament by Christian thinkers and teachers in the pre-literary period. What we are trying to do is to get an opening into the intellectual workshop of the early Church, and to watch its mind at work.

Our first task will be to collect passages from the Old Testament which, being cited by two or more writers of the New Testament in *prima facie* independence of one another, may fairly be presumed to have been current as *testimonia* before they wrote.

Two points should first be cleared up with regard to method. The first has to do with the question of the independence of writers over against one another. In much criticism of an earlier day the general presumption was entertained that the writings of the New Testament formed a series which, when arranged in correct chronological order, would reveal a more or less orderly development, in which each would show dependence on its predecessor, and each would be seen to have exerted influence on its successor. It was of course recognized that the series could not be reconstructed in a complete form. Some of the links have not survived. But sometimes at least the critic found himself able to recover by probable arguments from the *data* a lost source which provided a missing link. Critical work carried out upon this hypothesis undoubtedly made important contributions to our understanding of early Christian history. But much of the new work done in the last half-century has gone to show that the picture was somewhat out of focus. The early Church was not such a bookish community. The main current of its life and thought seems to have been carried by oral tradition, at least to the end of the first century, and the surviving documents are, in large measure, the deposit of a common tradition in its various stages, developed in one way or another according to the idiosyncrasy of the several authors. In certain specific cases indeed there is definite evidence that writings had some kind of literary connection, over and above the common tradition underlying them all, but except where some such evidence can be adduced, the presumption of literary dependence is precarious, since resemblances might be so probably accounted for without it.

C

I shall therefore proceed upon the hypothesis that where two separate writers cite the same passage from the Old Testament, unless there are definite reasons to the contrary, they represent to that extent a common tradition. The hypothesis must be tested in each case on its merits. For our present purpose I shall treat the Pauline corpus (excluding Hebrews) as representing the work of one author. Even if certain of the writings contained in it may not be from the hand of the apostle, they all depend largely upon him. The two Lucan writings, again, the Third Gospel and the Acts of the Apostles, represent a single author. In works therefore belonging to either of these two groups coincidence in the citation of the Old Testament will carry, *prima facie*, no weight as evidence for pre-canonical tradition. In the Synoptic Gospels we have a more complex case. That there is some degree of literary dependence among them seems certain, though it may sometimes be by way of a common written source no longer extant. It would be hazardous to assume that common citations in two or more of these gospels are made in genuine independence even though we may sometimes suspect that this is in fact the case. The Fourth Gospel on the other hand stands apart. All recent criticism tends to reduce the area of its dependence on the Synoptics to a small compass, if it does not discount it altogether, and citations common to the Synoptics on the one hand and the Fourth Gospel on the other are *prima facie* independent. As for the rest, the Epistle to the Hebrews appears to stand substantially apart from all other writings, even though its author may have been under the influence of Paul in certain respects, and the First Epistle of Peter does not at any rate afford such unmistakable evidence of derivation from the Pauline epistles that we must rule out independence from the outset. I shall treat it as *prima facie* independent, and investigate its citations to see how far this hypothesis is justified in particular cases. The Apocalypse stands very much alone, though it has problematic relations of some kind with other Johannine writings. It is deliberately moulded upon the model of earlier apocalyptic writings and so much of it is almost a *cento* of passages from parts of the Old Testament that its evidence is not for the most part of immediate relevance for the study of *testimonia*, though occasionally it may be treated as an independent witness. The remaining writings are not of great importance for our immediate purpose.

The second point which needs clearing up is the identification of quoted matter. The solid nucleus of our material consists of places where phrases, sentences or paragraphs from the Old Testament are introduced with a formula of quotation: "it is written," "that which was spoken by the prophet," or the like. But there are many other places where the intention to quote is evident, though no formula of quotation is employed. Such passages show all degrees of resemblance to the text of the Old Testament—verbal identity with the manuscript text of the LXX, alternative translation of the Hebrew original, paraphrase, or a similarity just sufficient to suggest an allusion. It is sometimes a delicate matter to be sure that an allusion is intended, but if the allusion is clear, even though there is no explicit indication that the Old Testament is being cited, the passage must be included. The reasons for doing so will become stronger as the argument proceeds.

With this preface I proceed to a list of *testimonia*.

1. Ps. ii. 7: "Thou art my son; this day have I begotten thee."

This passage is cited, with the rubric, "it is written in

the second psalm," in Acts xiii. 33. In Heb. i. 5 and v. 5 it
is quoted as what God "said," or "spoke" (τίνι εἶπεν, i. 5;
ὁ λαλήσας, v. 5). Without a formula of quotation the same
passage is probably to be recognized in Mk. i. 11, where
however the second clause is absent, and it perhaps
underlies Mk. ix. 7, Mt. iii. 17. In Lk. iii. 22 the "western
text" has the entire passage, exactly as in the LXX. This
is probably secondary, but it is conceivable that Luke
gave the full form here as in Acts xiii. 33, and that the
prevailing textual tradition assimilated it to Mk. i. 11.
It is thus fairly clear that three authors at least employ
Ps. ii. 7 as a *testimonium* to the messiahship of Jesus; that
is, as documentation of one of the main themes of the
kerygma. In all probability they do so without literary
dependence upon one another, and we may reasonably infer
a pre-canonical employment of the passage in that sense.

2. Ps. viii. 4-6: "What is man, that thou art mindful of
him, or the son of man that thou visitest him? Thou
madest him for a little while inferior to the angels; thou
crownedst him with glory and honour; thou didst set him
over the works of thy hands; thou didst put all things
under his feet" (so LXX).

The whole passage is quoted in Heb. ii. 6-8, in a form
identical with the MS. text of the LXX, except that the
clause "thou didst set him over the works of thy hands"
is omitted. The rubric is διεμαρτύρατό πού τις λέγων, a
type of quotation-formula characteristic of this author,
with his addiction to rhetorical elegance. In I Cor. xv. 27
the words "he put all things under his feet" are clearly
intended as a citation of our passage, since Paul continues,
ὅταν εἴπῃ ὅτι πάντα ὑποτέτακται. . . . He is here arguing
that even death will be subdued to Christ. His authority
for this is the statement in Ps. viii. 6 that *all* things are
by divine decree subordinated to the "Son of Man."

The implication is that this scripture will be recognized as referring to Christ. The same passage is again alluded to, without formula of quotation, in Eph. i. 22, again in the form "He put all things under his feet". Phil. iii. 21, τοῦ δύνασθαι αὐτὸν καὶ ὑποτάξαι αὐτῷ τὰ πάντα is also probably to be regarded as another allusion. The argument here is as follows: it is perfectly possible for God to accomplish the miracle of transforming our bodies into the likeness of his glory, since (as we know from scripture) He is able to subject all things to Christ. This argument becomes perspicuous if we assume that Paul saw in the triumph of Christ over death the pledge of glory for mankind as such, to which the psalm refers. The promise of Ps. viii that man, in the person of Him who is "Son of man" (or in Pauline terms, the Man from heaven) shall be crowned with glory and honour, has been fulfilled in Christ, and will be fulfilled for those who are "in Him." But all this is so implicit that we should naturally conclude that Paul was basing himself on an accepted interpretation of scripture. That he owed this interpretation to the Epistle to the Hebrews is most improbable. The probability is that he and the author to the Hebrews follow a common tradition.

Again, we probably have an allusion to the same verse in I Pet. iii. 22, ὑποταγέντων αὐτῷ ἀγγέλων. The theme of Ps. viii. 4-6, as understood by Christians, is that Christ (as "Son of Man") was temporarily reduced to a status inferior to that of the angels, only to be raised to sovereignty over all beings, including, of course, the angels to whom he was formerly inferior. This understanding of the psalm would supply scriptural authority for the statement made in I Pet. iii. 22. It seems probable, therefore, that the author of this work is following, once again, an accepted interpretation of the psalm. There is nothing to suggest that he took it from Paul, or from Hebrews. There is at any rate a high degree of probability that three authors have gone back to this particular scripture, in different contexts, because it was already accepted as a *testimonium* to Christ before any of them wrote. It supplies scriptural documentation for the Christian affirmation that "the Messiah must suffer and enter into his glory" (Lk. xxiv. 26).

It seems just possible that we may trace the remoter influence of this *testimonium* in the hymn to Christ which appears in Rev. v. 12: "Worthy is the slain Lamb to receive power and wealth and wisdom and strength and *honour and glory* and blessing." If we reflect that the psalm (in its Christian reference) speaks of the glory and honour which accrue to Christ *after His humiliation*, and that the author to the Hebrews expressly asserts that it came to him διὰ τὸ πάθημα τοῦ θανάτου, it will appear not impossible that the conception of δόξα καὶ τιμή as the conspicuous prerogatives of the Crucified should have sunk so deeply into the imagination of the Church that it came to expression alike in theological argument and in hymns of worship—in the latter, expanded with a series of other attributes in the manner of the "plerophory" characteristic of liturgical language. But upon this I lay no stress. It serves only to keep in view the extensive area over which we must be prepared to find the spreading effects of the Church's early preoccupation with the language of the Old Testament.

3. Ps. cx. 1 (LXX, cix. 1): "The Lord said to my lord, Sit thou at my right hand until I make thy enemies the footstool of thy feet."

This is expressly cited in Acts ii. 34-35, after the MS. text of the LXX, under the rubric, "David himself says." In Mk. xii. 36 it is cited, with one unimportant variation from the LXX text, under the rubric, "David himself said in the holy Spirit." In Heb. i. 13 the words κάθου ἐκ δεξιῶν μου ἕως ἂν θῶ τοὺς ἐχθρούς σου ὑποπόδιον τῶν ποδῶν σου are cited without express formula of citation, but with the introduction, πρὸς τίνα τῶν ἀγγέλων εἴρηκέν ποτε; which comes as near to such a formula as need be. Thus we may claim three direct witnesses to the primitive use of this passage as a *testimonium*.

But allusions to this verse are numerous throughout the New Testament. Thus Mk. xiv. 62 speaks of the Son of Man ἐκ δεξιῶν καθήμενον τῆς δυνάμεως. In Acts vii. 55 the dying Stephen sees the Son of Man ἐκ δεξιῶν ἐστῶτα[1] τοῦ θεοῦ. In Rom. viii. 34, where Paul is briefly enumerating the central facts of the *kerygma*, we have "Christ Jesus, who died, or rather who rose again, and who is at the right hand of God." Similar echoes of the psalm are found in Eph. i. 20 and Col. iii. 1; and in Hebrews, apart from the express citation in i. 13, the expression, "seated at the right hand of God," or the like, is found in i. 3, viii. 1, x. 12, xii. 2. In I Pet. iii. 22 once again we have a reference to the resurrection of Christ, followed immediately by the words, "who is at the right hand of God." It seems clear, therefore, that this particular verse was one of the fundamental texts of the *kerygma*, underlying almost all the various developments of it, and cited independently in Mark, Acts, Paul, Hebrews and I Peter.

4. Ps. cxviii. (LXX, cxvii). 22-23: "The stone which the builders rejected has become the top of the pediment. This is from the Lord, and it is marvellous in our eyes."

---

[1] It is hardly likely that the substitution of the verb ἑστάναι for the καθῆσθαι of the LXX is significant, for ἑστάναι, like "stand" in English and עמד in Hebrew, has commonly the sense "to be situated," without any necessary implication of an upright attitude (*"se tenir débout"*).

This passage is cited in Mk. xii. 10-11, in a form verbally identical with the MS. text of the LXX, with the introduction, "Did you never read this scripture?" In I Pet. ii. 7 verse 22 alone is cited, as part of a *catena* of passages introduced by the formula, περιέχει ἐν γραφῇ. There is a clear allusion to it, though without express marks of citation, in the kerygmatic passage Acts. iv. 11: "This is the stone which was rejected by you builders and has become the top of the pediment." We have therefore threefold witness to the use of this passage as a *testimonium*. The evidence will appear even stronger when we come to consider how it is combined with other passages in various writers.

5. Is. vi. 9-10: "You shall hear and hear, but never understand, look and look but never see. The heart of this people has grown gross, their ears are dull of hearing, and they have closed their eyes, lest they should see with their eyes and hear with their ears, and understand with their hearts, and should be converted, and I should heal them."

This passage is quoted at length, in a form verbally identical with the א text of the LXX, in Matthew xiii. 14-15, under the rubric, ἀναπληροῦται ἡ προφητεία Ἡσαΐου ἡ λέγουσα. It is again cited in Acts xxviii. 25-27, in identical form, but with the addition of the words of introduction, in a form differing unimportantly from the LXX, πορεύθητι πρὸς τὸν λαὸν τοῦτον καὶ εἰπόν.

In Jn. xii. 40 part of the passage is cited, under the rubric, "Again Isaiah said," and with the additional note, ταῦτα εἶπεν Ἡσαΐας ὅτι εἶδεν τὸν δόξαν αὐτοῦ. (So א, B, Θ, etc.), which is an implicit reference to vi. 1.[1] The reading

---

[1] The substitution of εἶδεν τὴν δόξαν for Isaiah's blunt εἶδον τὸν κύριον is in line with the general practice of "reverential periphrasis," though in this case it is directly justified by the reference to δόξα which immediately follows in the latter part of the same verse.

of T.R., ὅτε εἶδεν, would amount to an explicit indication
of the context, as much as to say "in chapter vi," where
Isaiah's vision is described. The form, however, in which
the quotation is given differs widely from the LXX text.
The two forms are as follows:

LXX	JN. XII
ἐπαχύνθη ἡ καρδία τοῦ λαοῦ τούτου	τετύφλωκεν[1] αὐτῶν τοὺς ὀφθαλμούς
. . . καὶ τοὺς ὀφθαλμοὺς ἐκάμμυσαν	καὶ ἐπώρωσεν[2] αὐτῶν τὴν καρδίαν
μή ποτε ἴδωσιν τοῖς ὀφθαλμοῖς . . .	ἵνα μὴ ἴδωσιν τοῖς ὀφθαλμοῖς
καὶ τῇ καρδίᾳ συνῶσιν καὶ ἐπιστρέψωσιν	καὶ νοήσωσιν τῇ καρδίᾳ καὶ στραφῶσιν
καὶ ἰάσομαι αὐτούς	καὶ ἰάσομαι αὐτούς

In Mk. iv. 12 (followed by Lk. viii. 10) we have a clear
citation of the same passage, though without any express
formula of quotation, in a form which differs both from
the LXX (Matthew and Acts) and from John:

LXX	MK. IV
ἀκοῇ ἀκούσετε καὶ οὐ μή συνῆτε	ἵνα βλέποντες βλέπωσιν καὶ μὴ ἴδωσιν
καὶ βλέποντες βλέψετε καὶ οὐ μὴ ἴδητε	καὶ ἀκούοντες ἀκούωσιν καὶ μὴ συνιῶσιν
. . . μή ποτε . . . ἐπιστρέψωσιν καὶ ἰάσομαι αὐτούς	μή ποτε ἐπιστρέψωσιν καὶ ἀφεθῇ αὐτοῖς

[1] Τυφλοῦν is found in LXX only in Tob. vii. 7 and Wisd. ii. 21, in both
of which places there are variants, and in Is. xlii.19, ἐτύφλωσαν οἱ δοῦλοι
τοῦ θεοῦ.

[2] Πωροῦν is found in two passages only of the LXX, in both of which
there are variants, Job. xvii. 7 (v. l, πεπήρωνται), and Prov. x. 20 (v. l,
πεπυρωμένος). It is not to be thought that either of these passages
can have influenced New Testament writers in their citation of Isaiah vi.

In view of these striking differences of translation, it is not plausible to suppose that these authors were borrowing from one another. We are clearly dealing with independent citations of the same passage.

The version which underlies the Johannine form of citation, implying a "judicial blinding" of rebellious Israel, seems to find a clear echo in another passage of the same gospel, ix. 39, where Jesus declares, "for judgment I have come into the world, ἵνα οἱ μὴ βλέποντες βλέπωσιν καὶ οἱ βλέποντες τυφλοὶ γένωνται." The companion expression, ἐπώρωσεν αὐτῶν τὴν καρδίαν, finds no echo elsewhere in the Fourth Gospel, but it seems to be implied in several passages of Mark, viz. iii. 5, ἡ πώρωσις τῆς καρδίας αὐτῶν, vi. 52, ἦν αὐτῶν ἡ καρδία πεπωρωμένη, viii. 17, πεπωρωμένην ἔχετε τὴν καρδίαν ὑμῶν; In the last of these places it is associated with a reminiscence of Jer. v. 21, or the closely similar Ezek. xii. 2: ὀφθαλμοὺς ἔχοντες οὐ βλέπετε καὶ ὦτα ἔχοντες οὐκ ἀκούετε; Both of these prophecies have some resemblance to Is. vi. 10. Further, in Rom. xi. 7-8 the verb πωροῦν is again associated with the idea of eyes that do not see and ears that do not hear, and this is, once again, probably a reminiscence either of Is. vi. 10 or of the similar passages of Jeremiah and Ezekiel. This certainly suggests that some version of Isaiah vi similar to that used by the Fourth Evangelist may have been known to Paul. Consider again II Cor. iii. 14, ἐπωρώθη τὰ νοήματα, with II Cor. iv. 4, ἐτύφλωσεν τὰ νοήματα τῶν ἀπίστων. Though here the blinding is attributed to "the god of this aeon," yet the association of πωροῦν with τυφλοῦν is suggestive. The πώρωσις καρδίας appears yet again in Eph. iv. 18.

In view of all this it seems highly probable that Is. vi. 10 was widely accepted at an early period as a *testimonium* to the situation which arose when the Jews rejected the Gospel and were found to be excluded from the new people of God, and that it was employed as such in more versions than one, the most influential being a non-Septuagintal version known to Paul and John and possibly to Mark. It was clearly regarded as, constructively, providing documentation for the thesis that the Gospel is to be preached to the Gentiles, and in that sense obviously had great importance for primitive Christian apologetic.

6. Is. liii. 1: "Lord, who believed our report, and to whom was the arm of the Lord revealed?"

This passage is quoted, exactly as it stands in the MS. text of the LXX, in Jn. xii. 38, under the rubric, "The word of Isaiah the prophet, which he spoke." The first clause alone, in the same form, is quoted by Paul in Rom. x. 16, introduced by the formula "Isaiah says." That Paul had read the Fourth Gospel is impossible, and that the Fourth Evangelist had read the Epistle to the Romans would be a conjecture for which no evidence can be adduced. It is a reasonable inference that both writers employed a *testimonium* already recognized.

7. Is. xl. 3-5: "A voice of one crying in the wilderness: Prepare the way of the Lord, make straight the paths of our God. Every valley shall be filled in, and every mountain and hill be made low. All crooked places shall be made straight, the rough shall be made level, and the glory of the Lord shall appear and all flesh shall see the salvation of our God" (so LXX).

This passage is quoted *in extenso* in Lk. iii. 4-6, under the rubric, "It is written in the Book of Isaiah the prophet." Luke follows the A text of the LXX fairly closely, reading however αὐτοῦ for τοῦ θεοῦ ἡμῶν, and αἱ τραχεῖαι for ἡ τραχεία, and omitting the clause καί ὀφθήσεται ἡ δόξα κυρίου.

The opening clauses, φωνή βοῶντος ἐν τῇ ἐρήμῳ, Ἑτοιμάσατε τὴν ὁδὸν κυρίου, εὐθείας ποιεῖτε τὰς τρίβους αὐτοῦ, exactly as in Luke, are quoted in Mt. iii. 3, introduced by the formula, Οὗτός ἐστιν ὁ ῥηθεὶς διὰ Ἡσαΐου τοῦ προφήτου λέγοντος, and again in Mk. i. 3, conflated with Mal. iii. 1, the whole conflate quotation being introduced by the words, "as it is written in Isaiah the prophet."

In Jn. i. 23 the opening words are given in a slightly different form, φωνὴ βοῶντος ἐν τῇ ἐρήμῳ, Εὐθύνατε τὴν ὁδὸν κυρίου, with the note, "as Isaiah the prophet said." Those who assume the older view that the Fourth Gospel is fundamentally dependent on the Synoptics will no doubt regard the quotation as having been borrowed from Mark or one of the others; but they will have to explain how it is that John gives a different translation, for he has not drawn it from the LXX. This is in favour of John's independence at this point. If it be granted that John accepted this passage as a *testimonium*, independently of any borrowing from the Synoptics, it will perhaps appear not entirely improbable that the same passage is echoed in two other places of the Fourth Gospel. The LXX of Is. xl. 5 gives ὀφθήσεται ἡ δόξα κυρίου καὶ ὄψεται πᾶσα σὰρξ τὸ σωτήριον τοῦ θεοῦ. There may be possible reminiscences of these clauses in Jn. xi. 40, ὄψῃ τὴν δόξαν τοῦ θεοῦ, and perhaps i. 14, ἐθεασάμεθα τὴν δόξαν αὐτοῦ. If so, then the evangelist was not following the Synoptics here, since the clause ὀφθήσεται ἡ δόξα κυρίου is the one omitted in Luke, and neither of the others has this part of the quotation. I lay no stress on this suggestion, though as the argument advances it will perhaps be thought less improbable than it seems at this point. But I should submit that the agreement of John and the Synoptics in treating this passage as a *testimonium* is probable evidence of its employment as such in the pre-canonical tradition.

Whether the agreement of the Synoptic Gospels in citing this passage has any particular significance is not clear. Where the three agree, we usually assume that Matthew and Luke are following Mark. If this is so in the present case, we must assume that both of them independently disentangled the two quotations which Mark has conflated, and that Luke in addition turned to his LXX to complete a quotation of which Mark had given only part. This is not unlikely in itself, yet many critics have suspected that Matthew and Luke here had a second source in which Isaiah xl. 3-5 and Mal. iii. 1 appeared separately (cf. Matthew xi. 10). Some slight support for the view that Luke followed some tradition (written or oral) besides Mark in referring to this passage of Isaiah may be found in the clear echo of the same passage in the *Nunc Dimittis*, εἶδον οἱ ὀφθαλμοί μου τὸ σωτήριόν σου. In any case we may accept Lk. ii. 30 as a third independent appearance of this *testimonium*.

Thus, while the argument for this passage is perhaps not quite so strong as for the passages we have previously considered, there appears to be a reasonably high degree of probability that it is to be added to the list of passages recognized as *testimonia* in the pre-canonical tradition.

8. Is. xxviii. 16: "Behold I lay in Zion for a foundation a stone, a tried stone, a precious corner stone of sure foundation: he that believeth shall not make haste" (I give here the R.V. rendering, which is not a perfect translation of the Hebrew text, but will serve for reference; the LXX differs); and Is. viii. 14: "a stone of stumbling and a rock of offence."

These two passages are quoted in I Pet. ii. 6, 8, as part of a *catena* of citations introduced by the formula, περιέχει ἐν γραφῇ. They are not in immediate contiguity, being separated by the quotation of Ps. cxviii. 22-23 (No. 4 above). Neither is quoted exactly after the LXX.

Is. xxviii. 16 runs as follows in the two versions:

LXX ℵA	I PET.
ἰδοὺ ἐμβαλῶ εἰς τὰ θεμέλια Σιὼν	ἰδοὺ τίθημι ἐν Σιὼν
λίθον πολυτελῆ ἐκλεκτὸν	λίθον ἐκλεκτὸν
ἀκρογωνιαῖον ἔντιμον, εἰς τὰ θεμέλια αὐτῆς	ἀκρογωνιαῖον ἔντιμον
καὶ ὁ πιστεύων ἐπ᾽ αὐτῷ	καὶ ὁ πιστεύων ἐπ᾽ αὐτῷ
οὐ μὴ καταισχυνθῇ	οὐ μὴ καταισχυνθῇ

Is. viii. 14 runs as follows:

LXX	I PET.
οὐχ ὡς λίθου προσκόμματι συναντήσεσθε	λίθος προσκόμματος
οὐδὲ ὡς πέτρας πτώματι	καὶ πέτρα σκανδάλου

In Rom. ix. 33 the same two passages are conflated: ἰδοὺ τίθημι ἐν Σιὼν λίθον προσκόμματος καὶ πέτραν σκανδάλου, καὶ ὁ πιστεύων ἐπ᾽ αὐτῷ οὐ καταισχυνθήσεται. So far as this abbreviated form of quotation can be compared, it agrees with the LXX and differs from it precisely as does I Peter, except that οὐ καταισχυνθήσεται takes the place of οὐ μὴ καταισχυνθῇ. In particular, both agree in giving the correct rendering of the Hebrew, λίθος προσκόμματος and πέτρα σκανδάλου, for the incorrect LXX rendering.[1] This agreement can hardly be fortuitous. Yet the hypothesis of literary interdependence is attended with difficulty. That Paul borrowed from I Peter few would be found to maintain, even among those who

[1] Moreover, while the LXX *denies* the πρόσκομμα and the πτῶμα, Peter and Paul seem to presuppose a text which *affirmed* the actuality of both.

assign I Peter to the earliest date possible. That the
author of I Peter borrowed from Romans could be maintained only on the rather unlikely assumption that he first
disentangled the conflated passages, and then supple-
mented them with parts of Is. xxviii. 16 which Paul had
omitted, and yet that he did not supplement them out
of the LXX, since his version does not entirely agree
with the LXX even where there is no Pauline parallel.
The simpler, and surely the more probable, hypothesis is
that both Paul and the author of I Peter made use of a
twofold *testimonium* already current in the pre-canonical
tradition in a version differing somewhat from the LXX.

9. Gen. xii. 3: "In thee shall all the tribes of the earth
be blessed"; and Gen. xxii. 18: "In thy seed shall all the
nations be blessed." (I translate both these passages after
the LXX. It does not accurately represent the meaning of
the Hebrew, since נִבְרְכוּ is properly reflexive, and the
meaning should apparently be, "shall bless themselves";
i.e. shall pray to be blessed as Abraham was blessed. But
there is no trace of any apprehension of this meaning
either in the LXX or in the New Testament).

These two passages are conflated in two places. In Acts
iii. 25, following closely upon the statement that "these
days" had been foretold by all the prophets, we have a
reference to the covenant which God made with the
patriarchs, "saying to Abraham, ἐν τῷ σπέρματί σου
ἐνευλογηθήσονται πᾶσαι αἱ πατριαὶ τῆς γῆς." The words
underlined come from Gen. xxii. 18 (with a change of
order); the remainder clearly represent πᾶσαι αἱ φυλαὶ τῆς
γῆς in Gen. xii. 3. In Gal. iii. 8 Paul cites from "scripture" (ἡ γραφή) the promise of God to Abraham,
ἐνευλογηθήσονται ἐν σοὶ πάντα τὰ ἔθνη. Here the words
underlined come from Gen. xii. 3, and the rest from Gen.

xxii. 18. Since Paul and the author of Acts have conflated the passages differently, we cannot suppose that the one borrowed from the other; but all would be intelligible if we assumed that the two passages were already accepted as *testimonia* in the pre-canonical tradition, and that our authors quoted somewhat carelessly what was extremely familiar. The importance of the prophecy is obvious, as documentation of the theme that the Gospel is to be preached to the Gentiles, and we can well believe that it was seized upon from the first by apologists for the Gentile mission.

10. Jer. xxxi (LXX, xxxviii). 31-34: "Behold the days are coming, says the Lord, when I will make with the house of Israel and with the house of Judah a new covenant, not like the covenant which I made with their fathers, in the day when I took them by the hand to lead them out of the land of Egypt; because they did not abide by my covenant, and so I cared for them no longer, says the Lord. For this is the covenant which I will make with the house of Israel after those days, says the Lord: putting my laws into their mind, I will also write them on their heart; and I will be a God to them, and they shall be a people to me. And they shall not teach everyone his fellow-citizen and everyone his brother, saying, 'Know the Lord'; because they will all know me, from little to great among them, because I will be gracious to their injustices and will no more remember their sins" (so LXX).

This passage is quoted *in extenso* in Heb. viii. 8-12, with the introduction, μεμφόμενος αὐτοὺς λέγει, which amounts to a formula of quotation. Hebrews follows the A text of the LXX with very little variation. This is the only place where the prophecy of the New Covenant is thus expressly quoted, but there are numerous places where there are more or less clear allusions to it. The

prophecy sets forth the main features of the promised
covenant as follows: (a) the law written on the heart;
(b) the intimate relation of God and His people; (c)
knowledge of God; and (d) forgiveness of sins. These
features crop up in various combinations in New Testament writers.

In II Cor. iii it is clear that Paul, although he does not
expressly cite Jeremiah, has the prophecy in mind. It is
echoed, not only in the διακόνους καινῆς διαθήκης of verse
6, and by implication in τῆς παλαιᾶς διαθήκης of verse 14,
but also in the ἐγγεγραμμένη ἐν ταῖς καρδίαις of verse
2, which refers to clause (a) of the covenant, though
the expansion of this in verse 3 owes something to
Ezek. xi. 19; which contrasts καρδία λιθίνη with καρδία
σαρκίνη.

Again, I Cor. xi. 25 clearly alludes to the same prophecy
in describing the Cup of the Eucharist as διαθήκη καινὴ ἐν
τῷ αἵματί μου. The epithet καινή does not occur in other
accounts of the Words of Institution, apart from the
longer text of Luke xxii. 20, which may be dependent on
Paul. But in the Matthaean account, although the
adjective καινή is not present, the clause εἰς ἄφεσιν
ἁμαρτιῶν (Mt. xxvi. 28) recalls one of the main
features of the New Covenant in Jeremiah (d), and corresponds closely enough with the meaning of the Hebrew
אֶסְלַח לַעֲוֺנָם, although the LXX translates ἵλεως ἔσομαι.
It seems, therefore, that the association of the Jeremianic
New Covenant with the Eucharist is not peculiar to Paul,
and since he himself professes to be repeating a tradition
which he had received, we may with much probability
conclude that Jer. xxxi. 31 sqq. had affected the liturgical
tradition at a date earlier than the writing of I Corinthians.

The clause of the New Covenant, ἔσομαί αὐτοῖς εἰς

D

θεὸν καὶ αὐτοὶ ἔσονταί μοι εἰς λαόν (b) is included in a *catena* of Old Testament passages in II Cor. vi. 17-18, which also echoes Jer. xxxi. 9 (LXX, xxxviii. 9), ἐγενόμην τῷ Ἰσραὴλ εἰς πατέρα.

The clause of the covenant (c) which promises knowledge of God does not seem to be directly referred to in the New Testament, but it is perhaps hardly accidental that in I Jn. ii. 12-14, which sets forth the features of a state of existence when "the darkness is passing away and the light of reality is shining," couples closely the knowledge of God (c) and the forgiveness of sins (d); while we might find a remote echo of Jer. xxxi. 34 in the words of Jn. iv. 42: "We believe no longer on the strength of what you say, because we have heard for ourselves, and we know"; among the Samaritans it is no longer necessary for a man to teach his fellow-citizens, saying "Know the Lord."

Although, therefore, there is only one place where the prophecy of the New Covenant is expressly cited as from scripture, it seems clear that it was widely influential in the Church from an early date, since it has not only influenced Paul, Hebrews and the Synoptic tradition, and possibly the Johannine tradition too, but probably had a place in primitive liturgical forms.

11. Joel ii. 28-32: "After that it shall be that I pour out some of my spirit on all flesh; and your sons and daughters will prophesy, your elders will dream dreams, and your young men will see visions; and upon my slaves and bond-maids in those days I will pour some of my spirit. And I will give prodigies in heaven and upon the earth blood and fire and vapour of smoke. The sun will be changed to darkness and the moon to blood before the great and manifest day of the Lord comes. And it shall be that everyone who invokes the name of the Lord shall be saved. For in Mount Zion and in Jerusalem there shall be a saved

man, and there shall be men who preach the Gospel to those whom the Lord has called" (so LXX).

The first four-and-a-half verses of this passage (down to "shall be saved," 32a) are quoted *in extenso* in Acts ii. 17-21, under the rubric, "This is that which was spoken through the prophet Joel." The citation is completed by the clear allusion to verse 32c in Acts ii. 39.[1] The author of Acts has followed the text of the LXX as we have it in the MSS., with a few not very important variations. The citation forms the opening of the speech attributed to Peter on the Day of Pentecost—the first rendering of the apostolic *kerygma* in the Acts, presented as a kind of programme of the Christian mission. It seems clear, therefore, that this prophecy of Joel was an important *testimonium;* yet there is not very much direct evidence of its use outside Acts.

In Rom. x. 13 Paul cites the words, "Everyone who invokes the name of the Lord shall be saved," exactly as they stand in the LXX of Joel ii. 32a.[2] The citation occurs in a passage which is essentially a commentary (a kind of "Midrash") on certain passages of the Old Testament, most of which are introduced by such formulae as Μωυσῆς γράφει (5), λέγει ἡ γραφή (11), γέγραπται (15), Ἡσαΐας λέγει (16). It is thus a mere accident that no such formula happens to be used in verse 13; the intention to quote is clear. It is further to be observed that among the passages here cited occur two which we have already

[1] This should be noted as a clear indication that the scripture which a writer has in mind is not necessarily limited to the amount which he quotes. The quotation of Joel ends at Acts ii. 21 in the middle of verse 32, but the latter part of verse 32, "those whom the Lord has called" crops up at Acts ii. 39 in a way which shows that the whole passage was in mind. It is perhaps the clearest of many examples of the kind.

[2] The expression οἱ ἐπικαλούμενοι τὸ ὄνομα κυρίου has become for Paul a synonym for "Christians", the κύριος being, of course, "our Lord Jesus Christ," I Cor. i. 2.

noted as primitive *testimonia*, Is. xxviii. 16 (verse 11) and
Is. liii. 1 (verse 16); and if we go a little further, to xi. 8,
which still belongs to the same argument, we shall find
one of the passages about eyes that do not see and ears
that do not hear, which we have noted as being associated
with Is. vi. 10 as testimonies to the transference of the
privileges of the Gospel from the Jews to the Gentiles.
It seems clear that Paul is working largely with passages
from the Old Testament already current as *testimonia*, and
we need not hesitate to put down Joel ii. 32 among them.

For the rest, the language of Joel ii. 31 seems to have
had influence upon the apocalyptic conceptions of early
Christianity. It is echoed in Lk. xxi. 25, ἔσονται σημεῖα ἐν
ἡλίῳ καὶ σελήνῃ, Mk. xiii. 24, ὁ ἥλιος σκοτισθήσεται καὶ ἡ
σελήνη οὐ δώσει τo φέγγος αὐτῆς, Rev. ix. 2, ἐσκοτίσθη
ὁ ἥλιος (cf. reference to καπνός, though this looks back
also to Exod. xix. 18, and perhaps Gen. xix. 28). But all
this is little to our present purpose.

The use of this prophecy of Joel in Rom. x seems just
sufficient to justify the conclusion that its introduction
as a main *testimonium* to the *kerygma* in Acts ii is not due
to the author, but rests upon primitive (pre-Pauline)
usage.

12. Zech. ix. 9: "Rejoice greatly, O daughter of Zion;
shout, O daughter of Jerusalem: behold, thy king cometh
unto thee; he is just and having salvation; lowly, and riding upon an ass, even upon a colt the foal of an ass" (I give
the R.V. for convenience).

This is cited in Mt. xxi. 5, in a version approximating
to the LXX, under the rubric, "That which was spoken
through the prophet" and in Jn. xii. 15, in a different
and much abbreviated version, under the rubric, "As it is
written." The differences may be exhibited as follows:

LXX	MT.	JN.
Χαῖρε σφόδρα, θύγατερ Σειών κήρυσσε, θύγατερ Ἰερουσαλήμ	εἴπατε τῇ θυγατρὶ Σιών	μὴ φοβοῦ, θυγάτηρ Σιών
ἰδού, ὁ βασιλεύς σου ἔρχεταί σοι	ἰδοὺ ὁ βασιλεὺς σου ἔρχεταί σοι	ἰδοὺ ὁ βασιλεύς σου ἔρχεται
πραΰς καὶ ἐπιβεβηκὼς ἐπὶ ὑποζύγιον καὶ πῶλον νέον	πραΰς καὶ ἐπιβεβηκὼς ἐπὶ ὄνον καὶ ἐπὶ πῶλον υἱὸν ὑποζυγίου	καθήμενος ἐπὶ πῶλον ὄνου

The wide differences between the two forms of quotation, neither of which could be accounted for by the hypothesis of a revision on the basis of the LXX, make it entirely improbable that either evangelist was indebted to the other. In Mark there is no trace of the wording of the prophecy, unless it be in the mere use of the terms πῶλος and βασιλεία, so that the common element could not be accounted for by the hypothesis that each was altering a Marcan prototype in a different way. We seem to have a true case of independent citation, surely on the basis of a common tradition of *testimonia* rather than of any written source.

13. Hab. ii. 3-4: "Coming he will come and will not delay. If anyone draws back my soul does not approve of him, but the righteous will live by my faith" (so LXX, not altogether acceptable as a rendering of the Hebrew of the Massoretic text).

This passage is quoted in Heb. x. 37-38. There is no formula of quotation, but the intention to quote seems plain. It clearly has the LXX, and not the Hebrew, behind it, but the author quotes somewhat freely:

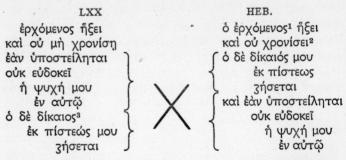

LXX

ἐρχόμενος ἥξει
καὶ οὐ μὴ χρονίσῃ
ἐὰν ὑποστείληται
οὐκ εὐδοκεῖ
ἡ ψυχή μου
ἐν αὐτῷ
ὁ δὲ δίκαιος[3]
ἐκ πίστεώς μου
ζήσεται

HEB.

ὁ ἐρχόμενος[1] ἥξει
καὶ οὐ χρονίσει[2]
ὁ δὲ δίκαιός μου
ἐκ πίστεως
ζήσεται
καὶ ἐὰν ὑποστείληται
οὐκ εὐδοκεῖ
ἡ ψυχή μου
ἐν αὐτῷ

In addition, he has prefixed to the passage from Habakkuk the words ἔτι γὰρ μικρὸν ὅσον ὅσον, which seem to be a reminiscence of Is. xxvi. 20, εἴσελθε εἰς τὰ ταμεῖά σου, ἀπόκλεισον τὴν θύραν σου, καὶ ἀποκρύβηθι μικρὸν ὅσον ὅσον, ἕως ἂν παρέλθῃ ἡ ὀργὴ κυρίου, a passage which, curiously enough, seems to be echoed also in Mt. vi. 6, but in a context which gives it no significance for our present purpose. This is no genuine case of conflation (like Nos. 8 and 9 above), where both passages have relevance to the matter in hand. It appears that the author is here quoting from memory.

One clause of the passage from Habakkuk is quoted by Paul in Rom. i. 17 and Gal. iii. 11. In the former place it is introduced by the formula, ὡς γέγραπται, and in the latter place it forms part of a series of quotations covered by similar formulae inserted at intervals. Paul's version of the clause differs both from the LXX and from Hebrews: ὁ δίκαιος ἐκ πίστεως ζήσεται, which he may have understood to mean "he who is righteous (i.e. "justified") by

---

[1] The expression, ὁ ἐρχόμενος, where LXX has ἐρχόμενος ἥξει (=בָּא יָבֹא), links itself with the use of the same phrase in Mt. xi. 3 =Lk. vii. 19, but whether the *testimonium* or the dialogue is prior we have no means of saying

[2] *v.l.* - ιεῖ

[3] +μου A

faith will come to life"[1] (in the sense of Rom. viii. 2).
That Paul borrowed from Hebrews is out of the question.
That the author of Hebrews borrowed from Paul is entirely unlikely, because (a) he gives the words differently;
(b) he cites much more of the passage, and (c) he evidently
understands the words differently; he quotes the whole
passage for the sake of its warning against ὑποστολή, and
treats πίστις as the opposite of the weakness of character
which leads to ὑποστολή (much more nearly in agreement
with the meaning intended by the prophet for the word
אֱמוּנָה). It is much more likely that he drew upon a
tradition which already recognized the passage from
Habakkuk as a *testimonium* to the coming of Christ, and
this tradition may well have been formed even before Paul
wrote to the Galatians; for his argument (which is very
much an *argumentum ad hominem*) would be far more
effective with his Jewish-Christian antagonists if it was
already common ground between them that when the
Coming One should come, ὁ δίκαιος ἐκ πίστεως ζήσεται.
The exact exegesis of those words would be legitimate
matter for discussion. The variation between the Hebrew
(צַדִּיק בֶּאֱמוּנָתוֹ יִחְיֶה = "the righteous will live by his
steadfastness"), the LXX (= "the just will live by
my faithfulness"), and the form known to the author to
the Hebrews ("my righteous one will live by faith"), as
well as Paul's own version without the possessive pro-
noun,[2] is sufficient to show that there were differences of
view. Hence there is reasonable probability that Hab. ii. 3-4
should be added to our list of traditional *testimonia* from
the earliest period.

[1] If he had been writing freely, he might have given the form ὁ ἐκ
πίστεως δίκαιος, as in Rom. x. 6 he writes ἡ ἐκ πίστεως δικαιοσύνη.

[2] Not to mention the reading of Codex Alexandrinus of Habakkuk,
which gives the sense "my righteous one will live by my faithfulness."
This is a mixed reading, almost certainly secondary.

14. Is. lxi. 1-2: "The spirit of the Lord is upon me, because he has anointed me. He has sent me to preach the gospel to the poor, to heal the broken-hearted, to proclaim release to captives and recovery of sight to the blind; to cry the acceptable year of the Lord" (so LXX).

This passage is quoted *in extenso* in Lk. iv. 18-19, with an introductory formula which explicitly refers to the prophet Isaiah. The quotation follows the MS. text of the LXX in essentials, except that it introduces a clause which is not present in Is. lxi: ἀποστεῖλαι τεθραυσμένους ἐν ἀφέσει, which clearly echoes Is. lviii. 6.[1]

There is no other explicit citation of this passage, but there are unmistakable allusions to it. In Acts x. 38 the address of Peter to Cornelius, which is recognized as an early formulation of the *kerygma*,[2] includes the phrase, ἔχρισεν αὐτὸν ὁ θεὸς πνεύματι ἁγίῳ. Like other kerygmatic passages, this address is dominated by the idea of prophecy fulfilled, and indeed the expression, "To him all the prophets testify," (x. 43) may, in view of the general character of the *kerygma*, be extended by implication beyond its immediate application, to cover all allusions to the Old Testament in the context.

[1] This curious interpolation may be due to fortuitous association; yet it is hardly accidental that the intrusive clause is drawn from a chapter which is echoed elsewhere in the New Testament, Is. lviii. 6, σύνδεσμον ἀδικίας, is echoed in Acts viii. 23, in combination with χολὴ πικρίας from Deut. xxix. 18 (a passage echoed also in Heb. xii. 15). In the same chapter, Is. lviii, the description of the "fast" which God requires (verse 7), following immediately upon the "bond of iniquity" and the release of the "bruised," with its insistence on feeding the hungry, clothing the naked and receiving the homeless, is similar in purport, though not in language, to Mt. xxv. 35-36; and the interweaving of the ideas of φῶς, δόξα θεοῦ, δικαιοσύνη, in 8-10, leading to the promise ἔσται ὁ θεός σου μετὰ σου (cf "Immanuel") is a part of the background of much that meets us in the New Testament.

[2] See my book, *The Apostolic Preaching and its Developments* (second edition) pp. 27-28.

Again, in Mt. xi. 5 = Lk. vii. 22, the statement τυφλοὶ ἀναβλέπουσιν . . . καὶ πτωχοὶ εὐαγγελίζονται is intended to prove, by appeal to manifest facts, that Jesus is ὁ ἐρχόμενος, which means that his activity corresponds to the affirmations of the prophets concerning the good time coming. Implicitly, therefore, the clause in question is an allusion to Is. lxi. 1. In a similar spirit the concluding clause of Is. lxi. 2, which Luke has not included, παρακαλέσαι πάντας τοὺς πενθοῦντας, is echoed in the beatitude upon the mourners in Mt. v. 4.

Although, therefore, it is only in Lk. iv. 18-19 that Is. lxi. 1-2 is expressly quoted, it seems to be treated as a source of *testimonia* in the kerygmatic passage of Acts x, which almost certainly rests upon earlier tradition, and in the "Q" stratum of Matthew and Luke, which, whether or not it had the character of a documentary source, also represents an early independent tradition. Lk. iv. 18-19 may represent another independent tradition (Luke's "special source"), or it may be that the author has intentionally cited at length a passage which he found to be alluded to in various parts of the tradition known to him. In any case, although the attestation of this citation is rather more slender than it was for some of the other passages we have investigated, there is a reasonable probability that it should be added to our list of primitive *testimonia*.

15. Deut. xviii. 15, 19: "A prophet from among your brethren, like me, will the Lord your God raise up for you; him you shall hear . . . and the man who does not hear whatever that prophet says in my name, I will exact the penalty from him."

This passage is cited in Acts iii. 22-23, under the rubric "Moses said." The citation, however, does not

exactly follow the text of the LXX (which I have trans-
lated) but "telescopes" it, and remoulds the conclusion in
a way which recalls Lev. xxiii. 29.

LXX	ACTS

(Dt. xviii. 15,) προφήτην   προφήτην
ἐκ τῶν ἀδελφῶν   ὑμῖν ἀναστήσει κύριος
σου ὡς ἐμὲ   ὁ θεὸς
ἀναστήσει κύριος   ἐκ τῶν ἀδελφῶν
ὁ θεός σου σοί   ὑμῶν ὡς ἐμέ
     αὐτοῦ ἀκούσεσθε   αὐτοῦ ἀκούσεσθε
                                 κατὰ πάντα

19, καὶ ὁ ἄνθρωπος
ὃς ἐὰν μὴ ἀκούσῃ
ὅσα ἐὰν λαλήσῃ   ὅσα ἂν λαλήσῃ πρὸς ὑμᾶς
ἐγὼ ἐκδικήσω ἐξ αὐτοῦ
Lev. xxiii. 29, πᾶσα ψυχὴ   ἔσται δὲ πᾶσα ψυχὴ
     ἥτις μὴ   ἥτις ἐὰν μὴ
ταπεινωθήσεται

                              ἀκούσῃ τοῦ προφήτου
                                 ἐκείνου

ἐξολεθρευθήσεται   ἐξολεθρευθήσεται
ἐκ τοῦ λαοῦ αὐτῆς   ἐκ τοῦ λαοῦ

The combination of Deuteronomy and Leviticus must
be regarded as due to fortuitous association. It is no
genuine conflation, since the passage in Leviticus has no
bearing on the matter in hand. The author's intention
is clearly to quote the prophecy from Deuteronomy about
the prophet like Moses whom God is to raise up. The
essential clause is quoted again in Acts vii. 37, προφήτην
ὑμῖν ἀναστήσει ὁ θεὸς ἐκ τῶν ἀδελφῶν ὑμῶν ὡς ἐμέ, with
the introductory words, "This is the Moses who said to the
sons of Israel . . ." The whole of Stephen's address in

which the quotation occurs is something like a *cento* of passages from the Old Testament with comments upon them. The repeated occurrence of the same quotation *within the same work* has no necessary significance for our present purpose; but there is much to be said for the view that in the kerygmatic passages (to which Acts iii. 12-26 belongs) traditional material is being introduced,[1] and that Stephen's speech in Acts vii, which has a style and manner of its own, unlike anything else in Acts, may also go back to a pre-canonical source the nucleus of which may well have been the *catena* from the Old Testament. This is however rather more speculative than befits the present stage of the investigation.

Outside Acts there is no explicit quotation of the prophecy of the prophet like Moses; but there appear to be several allusions to it. In Lk. ix. 35 the *bath-qol* at the Transfiguration runs, οὗτός ἐστιν ὁ υἱός μου ὁ ἐκλελεγμένος· αὐτοῦ ἀκούετε. Having in mind the importance of the prophecy from Deuteronomy for the author of Luke-Acts, we are led to suppose that he intended his readers to see here a reference to it, and to infer that Jesus is to be identified with the prophet like Moses. So far, the repeated reference, in the same author, need not have any particular significance; but in fact the crucial phrase occurs also in Mark's story of the Transfiguration (ix. 7), whether or not this has been Luke's model—and there are certain divergences, especially the substitution of ὁ ἐκλελεγμένος for ὁ ἀγαπητός, which suggest that he may not have been entirely dependent on Mark. If then the words ἀκούετε αὐτοῦ be thought to indicate a reference to the prophecy, we have a genuine second attestation of its use as a *testimonium*. That the prophet

[1] See *The Apostolic Preaching and its Developments* (second edition), pp. 17-20.

like Moses is in mind becomes slightly more likely when
we recall that Moses has figured in the scene of the Transfiguration, and that as the voice is heard he disappears,
and Jesus alone is visible: Moses has gone: the prophet
like Moses remains, and it is he whom men are to hear,
as the prophecy declared.

It seems probable that we are to find here the basis
of the reference to ὁ προφήτης ὁ ἐρχόμενος εἰς τὸν
κόσμον in Jn. vi. 14. Jesus has just given bread to the
people, as Moses had given manna in the wilderness
(vi. 31). He is therefore hailed as the coming prophet like
Moses. Since we have evidence that the passage from
Deuteronomy belonged to the corpus of prophecies
attached to the *kerygma* (even though proof that it belonged to the *primitive* corpus of such prophecies may fall
short of being conclusive), it appears gratuitous to seek
an explanation for the Johannine idea of the "coming
prophet" in the doctrine of the one prophet who comes
in age after age—a doctrine found in Manichæan and
other sources, but in no Christian source earlier than
the spurious Clementines (which are not earlier, it appears,
than the third century). While, however, in Mark and
Luke the coming prophet is clearly identified with the
Son (the Messiah), John seems to treat him as only a
quasi-messianic figure; for John the Baptist is offered his
choice of the roles of Messiah, Elijah, or "the prophet"
and rejects them all in favour of the designation φωνὴ
βοῶντος ἐν τῇ ἐρήμῳ (i. 23-25). It appears therefore as
if the Fourth Evangelist were acquainted with the employment of Deut. xviii. 15 as a *testimonium* to the
messianic dignity of Jesus, but did not accept it as
such.

It is clear that the evidence here is weaker than in the
previous cases, but I think it is enough to establish some

measure of probability that the scripture about the prophet like Moses is to be added to our list of primitive *testimonia*.

Here then are fifteen instances where there are grounds, and in most of them strong grounds, for believing that New Testament writers were working upon a tradition in which certain passages of the Old Testament were treated as "testimonies" to the Gospel facts, or in other words as disclosing that "determinate counsel of God" which was fulfilled in those facts. There is one feature of these citations which must now be brought out. Where two or more New Testament writers agree in citing some particular text from the Old Testament, as they agree in the fifteen instances given in the above list, they do not necessarily agree in the precise extent of the matter quoted. One writer may quote a somewhat lengthy passage *in extenso*, while another may quote only a single clause, another perhaps a different clause; and sometimes the matter quoted by different writers may overlap without being coextensive. We have now to observe that there are other cases, not in the list, where adjacent or contiguous clauses are cited by different writers but, as it happens, no one quotes the complete passage.

A striking example is Ps. lxix. 9 (LXX, lxviii. 10): "The zeal of thy house will devour me, and the reproaches of those who reproach thee fell upon me" (so LXX). The first member of this distich, ὁ ζῆλος τοῦ οἴκου σου καταφάγεταί με, is quoted, exactly as it stands in the LXX, in Jn. ii. 17, under the rubric "It is written." The second member, οἱ ὀνειδισμοὶ τῶν ὀνειδιζόντων σε ἐπέπεσαν ἐπ' ἐμέ, again in the septuagintal text, is quoted in Rom. xv. 3, under the rubric, "As it is written." In

both cases it is assumed without argument that the
passage refers to Christ. Are we to believe that each
of these writers, neither acquainted with the other's
work, selected by accident the two halves of a single
verse for use as a "testimony"—and that from a psalm
which is not, in any obvious sense, "messianic"? Surely
it is more probable that both writers were guided by a
tradition in which this psalm was already referred to
Christ.

This probability is strengthened when we observe that
other verses of Ps. lxix are cited as *testimonia* elsewhere in the New Testament, as follows:

4. οἱ μισοῦντές με δωρεάν	cited (with slight verbal change) in Jn. xv. 25, under the rubric, ὁ λόγος ὁ ἐν τῷ νόμῳ αὐτῶν γεγραμμένος
21*a*. ἔδωκεν εἰς τὸ βρῶμά μου χολήν	recalled in Mt. xxvii. 34 (without explicit quotation).
21*b*. εἰς τὴν δίψαν μου ἐπότισέν με ὄξος	recalled in Mk. xv. 36, Jn. xix. 28 (with the note, ἵνα τελειωθῇ ἡ γραφή)
25. γενηθήτω ἡ ἔπαυλις αὐτῶν ἠρημωμένη, καὶ ἐν τοῖς σκηνώμασιν αὐτῶν μὴ ἔστω ὁ κατοικῶν	quoted, with the omission of 3 words and with a change from plural to singular, in Acts ii. 20, under the rubric, γέγραπται ἐν βίβλῳ ψαλμῶν[1].

---

[1] The significance of these citations of scripture in the speech of Peter
upon the election to a vacancy in the apostolate is, I think, not always
appreciated. The situation brought about by Judas's defection is represented as unexpected and unprovided for. Upon the basis of the

It can scarcely be accidental that five separate authors have turned to this particular psalm for *testimonia*, although they have selected different sentences for quotation.

It seems then that we drew the line unnecessarily narrowly in limiting our evidence to cases where a New Testament writer has quoted at least *some* of the same words from a passage of scripture as others have quoted. We must also admit as evidence for a pre-canonical use of such passages of scripture cases where two or more writers have quoted, or recalled, contiguous or adjacent sentences within a wider context. The investigation of such cases will be our next task. But meanwhile our study has surely created a certain presumption that New Testament writers were guided in their use of the Old Testament by certain agreed principles or conventions. It has also suggested that such guidance may not have taken the form of an anthology of single, isolated proof-texts, as

saying about the "twelve thrones" (Mt. xix. 28 = Lk. xxii. 30), the disciples had no doubt assumed that the chosen twelve constituted a permanent government in the "Israel of God." If one of the chosen twelve disappears, what is to be done? Peter first shows that there is a real vacancy in the government. The mere death of an apostle need not have created a vacancy: ἐν τῇ παλιγγενεσίᾳ he would be there to take his throne; but apostasy is a different matter. He then shows that scripture has provided for the occurrence of a vacancy, in Ps. lxix. For its relevance and cogency the citation requires that it shall be agreed that the Psalm refers to the rejection and sufferings of Christ, in which Judas had played his part among the enemies of God. He then shows that scripture has also provided for the filling of the vacancy, in Ps. cix. (LXX. cviii), 8: τὴν ἐπισκοπὴν αὐτοῦ λάβοι ἕτερος. This being granted, the meeting can proceed to an election, assured that it is not acting *ultra vires*. There is of course no means of proving that all this is not the work of the author of Acts, but it appears to me that no *Sitz in Leben* for such a piece of tradition is so natural or likely as the early days of perplexity. That a recollection of the essential element of procedure on so momentous an occasion should have been preserved in tradition is in no way improbable, however much the author of Acts may have written it up.

has often been supposed. It points rather to the hypothesis that there were some parts of scripture which were early recognized as appropriate sources from which *testimonia* might be drawn. This hypothesis has now to be tested.

III

THE BIBLE OF THE EARLY CHURCH

IN our search for well-attested examples of citation from the Old Testament which may be supposed to be drawn from pre-canonical tradition, we have seen reason to believe that the unit of reference was sometimes wider than the usually brief form of words actually quoted, and that the citation by different writers of adjacent or contiguous passages within a single context may be evidence of a common pre-canonical tradition, just as strong as agreement in the citation of a single phrase or sentence. Our next step, clearly, should be to examine, first, the contexts from which our fifteen attested common citations are drawn, and then similar contexts from which adjacent or contiguous extracts have been drawn by more than one writer, with the aim of defining, in each case, the probable extent of the context which for this purpose was treated as a unit of scripture. That we should be able to do so in all cases with precision, is not to be expected, but if we could isolate with approximate accuracy certain portions of the Old Testament which can be shown to have been commonly used as a source of *testimonia*, we should have before us a body of scripture which we might assume with reasonable certainty to have been used by the earliest Christian thinkers in their efforts to understand and commend the contents of the *kerygma*. It should be observed that our fifteen citations refer, in nearly every case, to essential articles of the apostolic preaching, and

can be related for the most part to the general headings
under which the author of Luke-Acts has repeatedly
placed the exposition of the scriptures in the early
Church (see pp. 15-18). In our further investigations this
general reference to kerygmatic themes will serve as a
guiding thread through what at this point threatens to
become an unmanageable multiplicity of citations and
allusions. The New Testament writers give us to understand that certain facts to which they attach extreme
importance happened "according to the scriptures."
The question is, "What scriptures, in particular?" We are
attempting to answer that question, with such approach
to precision as may be possible.

To follow the method suggested in detail, however,
would prove tedious, involving a good deal of repetition.
It seems better to exhibit the results of such an examination in a systematic form, with references which should
enable the reader to verify for himself the degree of
strength of the evidence. I give therefore a list of portions
of the Old Testament which appear to have been used by
preference in illustration of the themes of the *kerygma*,
arranged in four groups.

I. *Apocalyptic-eschatological Scriptures*

The principal portions of scripture here are Joel ii-iii
(iii-iv in Hebrew), Zechariah ix-xiv, and parts of Daniel.

The starting point is the long citation of Joel in Acts ii
(see pp. 46-48). The passage there quoted stands in the
middle of a long continuous prophecy upon the theme of
the Day of the Lord. It begins (ii. 1), "Sound a trumpet in
Zion, proclaim (κηρύξατε) in my holy mountain . . . that the
Day of the Lord is here: it is at hand." We recall that the
image of the trumpet-call has passed into the standing

symbolism of Christian eschatology (cf. I Cor. xv. 52;
I Thess. iv. 16; Rev. *passim*), that the verb κηρύσσειν has
acquired a specific connotation in Christian usage, and
that the ὅτι ἐγγύς of Joel is echoed repeatedly in the
New Testament. After a description of the destructive
forces which are to become the agents or instruments of
divine judgment on sinful Israel, the trumpet-call is
repeated, accompanied by the command (according to the
LXX), "assemble a people, sanctify an *ecclesia*, elect
presbyters" (ii. 15-16)—words which the early Church
can hardly have helped applying to its own situation.
This proclamation heralds the sequel to judgment in
divine blessing on a renewed people, to whom the promise
is given, "You shall eat and be filled," which seems to be
echoed both in the beatitude of Lk. vi. 21 and in the
gospel accounts of the feeding of the multitude. This
leads up to the promise of the Spirit which in Acts ii
Peter declares to be fulfilled. But the judgment on the
Gentiles is still to come. It is described in Chapter iii in
phraseology which finds many vague echoes in the New
Testament,[1] though it affords no example of close quotation apart from iii. 13, "Put in the sickle, because harvest
is here"—words which (in a non-septuagintal version) are
adapted to form the conclusion of the parable of seed and
harvest in Mk. iv. 29. If the whole passage be considered,
it will appear probable that it played a significant part in
moulding the language in which the early Church set forth

[1] Joel iii. 2 introduces a scene of the judgment of the Gentiles,
and this is described, there and in verses 11-12, in terms which are
echoed in the judgment-scene of Mt. xxv. 31-46; cf. especially Joel's
συνάξω πάντα τὰ ἔθνη with Matthew's συναχθήσονται ἔμπροσθεν αὐτοῦ
πάντα τὰ ἔθνη. Again, the phrase κηρύξατε ἐν τοῖς ἔθνεσιν (Joel iii. 9)
would have a significant ring in Christian ears. The darkening of sun
and stars (iii. 15) and the shaking of heaven and earth (16) may be
commonplaces of apocalyptic imagery, but at any rate they form part
of the picture both here and in kindred passages of the New Testament.

its convictions about what Christ had done and would yet do. See further my pamphlet *The Old Testament in the New* (Athlone Press, 1952), pp. 17-19.

The second half of the Book of Zechariah, chs. ix-xiv, has the character of an apocalypse, and while its component visions (like those of many apocalypses) are not easy to bring into a consistent scheme, it can be understood as setting forth a whole eschatological programme, many elements of which have been taken up in the New Testament.

We start with ix. 9, the picture of the King riding into Zion "upon an ass and upon the foal of an ass," expressly quoted in Mt. xxi. 5 and Jn. xii. 15, in different versions, neither of them septuagintal (see pp. 48-49). The prophecy continues with a reference to the "blood of the covenant," (11) and is probably one of the scriptures underlying the "words of institution" at the last supper (Mk. xiv. 24, though the primary source is probably Exod. xxiv. 8; cf. Heb. ix. 20, x. 29, xiii. 20). It then proclaims an advent of the Lord, heralded, once again, by the trumpet call (ix. 14). In what follows the sustained figure of the flock of the Lord which He visits and saves (ix. 16, x. 3) brings us again into the sphere of New Testament thought and language; still more the promise, "I will redeem them" (λυτρώσομαι αὐτούς, x. 8). In Chapter xi the image of shepherd and flock recurs, but there is no striking parallel to New Testament language until we reach the strange passage about "thirty pieces of silver" (xi. 13) in which Matthew has discovered a *testimonium* to the venal treachery of Judas (Mt. xxvii. 9, where it is combined with words from Jer. xxxii. 6-9). There is no reason to suppose that this belongs to the primitive corpus

of *testimonia*, but we may well believe that Matthew was
led to it because the whole passage of Zechariah was
already recognized as a source of testimonies. To proceed,
in ch. xii we encounter two passages which have supplied
testimonia: verse 3, which speaks of Jerusalem being
trodden down by the Gentiles (cf. Lk. xxi. 24) and verse
10, where after a reference to the outpouring of the Spirit
which recalls the prophecy of Joel, we have the enigmatic
words, "they shall look upon him whom they pierced" (10).
This is quoted in Jn. xix. 37, as from "another scripture."
In Rev. i. 7 there is a fuller but somewhat freer citation:
"every eye shall see him, and those who pierced him, and
all the tribes of earth (this from Zech. i. 14) shall mourn
over him." Both writers follow a correct version of the
Massoretic text, similar to that of Theodotion, and differing widely from the LXX, which apparently represents
a variant reading in the Hebrew. The probable conclusion
is that both were independently following a pre-canonical
tradition; and this passage might have been included in
the list of primary *testimonia*, but for the fact that the
authors of the Fourth Gospel and of the Apocalypse,
however different their standpoints, are both (in all
probability) Ephesian authors and share in some degree
a common background, so that we might conceivably
have before us a common Ephesian or "Johannine"
tradition rather than something strictly *gemeinchristlich*.
Since however the evidence is now accumulating that
the whole context is one which drew the attention
of writers in various traditions, we need not hesitate to
set this down as one more item in the common stock.

In Chapter xiii, the opening section, verses 1-6, shows
no contact with the New Testament, though verse 6 was
in later times associated with the passion of Christ. But
with verse 7 we come to an important *testimonium*:

"smite the shepherd and the sheep will be scattered"
(so the Hebrew). This is quoted (under the rubric, "it is
written") in Mk. xiv. 27, in a slightly variant form, which
is however still nearer to the Hebrew than to the LXX:
"I will smite the shepherd and the sheep will be scattered."
In the context the shepherd who is to be smitten is
apparently a leader of Israel, whose death is followed by a
drastic purge of the people, leaving only one-third to call
upon the name of the Lord and to be accepted as His
people. The language of verse 9, πυρώσω αὐτοὺς ὡς πυροῦ-
ται τὸ ἀργύριον καὶ δοκιμῶ αὐτοὺς ὡς δοκιμάζεται τὸ
χρυσίον, seems to be echoed in I Pet. i. 7, τὸ δοκίμιον ὑμῶν
τῆς πίστεως πολυτιμότερον χρυσίου τοῦ ἀπολλυμένου,
διὰ πυρὸς δὲ δοκιμαζομένου (cf. also iv. 12, τῇ πυρώσει
πρὸς πειρασμὸν), and the conclusion, "They shall invoke
my name and I will hear them; I will say, It is my people;
and they shall say, The Lord is my God," is closely
similar to other Old Testament passages which are cited
as *testimonia* (see Jerem. xxxi. 33, pp. 44-46, above;
Hosea ii. 23, pp. 74-78, below).

Chapter xiv describes an advent of the Lord upon the
Mount of Olives, in language which occasionally seems to
be echoed in the New Testament, notably so in verse 5,
ἥξει ὁ κύριος καὶ πάντες οἱ ἅγιοι μετ' αὐτοῦ, cf. I Thess.
iii. 13 ἐν τῇ παρουσίᾳ τοῦ κυρίου ἡμῶν Ἰησοῦ μετὰ πάντων
τῶν ἁγίων αὐτοῦ. The promise of "living water" flowing
out of Jerusalem (verse 8) may be among the scriptures
which suggested the use of that symbol in the Fourth
Gospel, particularly in Jn. vii. 38, especially since it is
associated, there as here, with the Feast of Tabernacles
(verse 16). Finally, the prediction (21) that when the Lord
comes "there will be no trader in the house of the
Lord" (if, as seems probable, the word כְּנַעֲנִי is to be so

understood, and not as "Canaanite") may underly Jn. ii. 16, μὴ ποιεῖτε τὸν οἶκον τοῦ πατρός μου οἶκον ἐμπορίου.

In Zech. ix-xiv, then, although explicit quotations are not very thick on the ground, yet, apart from express quotations, there are no very long tracts without *some* phrases which are alluded to, or echoed, in various parts of the New Testament, and it appears highly probable that the whole was one of the scriptures which from a very early time were adduced in illustration of the Gospel facts.

In the Book of Daniel, our starting point will be the prophecy of the "Son of Man" in vii. 13. Although there is no explicit quotation of this passage, it is unmistakably in view in Mk. xiii. 26, xiv. 62, where it is conflated with Ps. cx. i, and Rev. i. 7, where it is associated with Zech. xii. 10. In Rev. i. 13 the same passage is employed in a different way, to supply, along with extracts from other Old Testament passages, details of the vision of Christ in glory; its employment in that way would not in itself be significant for our purpose. The coming of Christ "with clouds" is also implied in Acts i. 9-11, where the disciples, having seen Christ ascending in a cloud, are assured that He will come again "in the same manner," and in I Thess. iv. 17, where Christians who survive until Christ's second advent join the resurrected dead "in the clouds," to "meet the Lord in the air." This passage therefore is clearly one of those which from a very early stage were determinative of the manner in which Christians spoke and thought of that article of the *kerygma* which referred to the return of Christ as Judge and Saviour of men.

There are some further indications that this chapter was much in the mind of early Christian thinkers. In the interpretation of the vision the coming of the Son of Man signifies that God "has given the judgment to the saints of the Most High" (vii. 22), and this supplies the implicit scriptural authority for Paul's doctrine that "the saints shall judge the world" (I Cor. vi. 2). The equivalent expression "the saints of the Most High shall take over the kingdom" (Dan. vii. 18) is similarly echoed, not only in the hymn of Christ and the Church in Rev. v. 9-10, but also, ironically, in I Cor. iv. 8. The "faithful saying" of II Tim. ii. 11-12, apparently from a confession of faith in the form of a hymn, expresses the ultimate Christian formulation of the meaning of the vision, in which the Son of Man is at once Christ Himself, and the Church as the "people of the saints of the Most High": "If we endure, we shall also reign with him."

The same chapter of Daniel has some striking echoes in dominical sayings reported in the Gospels. In Lk. xxii. 28-30 the idea expressed concisely in the "faithful saying" appears in an extended form: "You are those who have stood by me in my trials; and as my Father has assigned a kingdom to me, so I assign to you the privilege of eating and drinking at my table in my kingdom; and you shall sit on thrones judging the twelve tribes of Israel." Mt. xix. 28 has the same saying in briefer form. The "thrones" figure in Dan. vii. 9,[1] and the twelve, as the nucleus of the new people of God, represent the "saints" to whom judgment is given. It is possible that Lk. xxii. 29 (which I believe, on the whole, should be construed as my translation indicates) might be construed with βασιλείαν as the direct object of the verb, so that we should have a statement, after Dan. vii. 18, that the

---

[1] There is evidence of discussion in Jewish rabbinical circles of the question, Why the plural "thrones"? Here, it seems, is the Christian answer. See Moore, *Judaism*, II, pp. 336-37.

kingdom is given to the saints. In any case this is directly
stated in Lk. xii. 32: "Fear not, little flock; it is your
Father's good pleasure to give you the kingdom." Most
striking of all perhaps is the allusion to Dan. vii. 22[1] in
the summary of the first proclamation of the Kingdom of
God by Jesus in Galilee, in Mk. i. 15.

DAN.	MK.
ὁ καιρὸς ἔφθασεν[2]	πεπλήρωται ὁ καιρός
καὶ τὴν βασιλείαν κατέσχον	καὶ ἤγγικεν[2] ἡ βασιλεία τοῦ
οἱ ἅγιοι	θεοῦ

There is amply enough here to show how deeply this
chapter of Daniel is embedded in the foundations of New
Testament thought.

There is one slight indication that some early Christian
thinkers at least were aware that the vision of the Son of
Man is in some sort parallel to the vision of the great image
in Dan. ii, where the various parts of the image are
equivalent to the four beasts, and the victorious people
of God (or Son of Man) appears as the "stone cut without
hands" which wrecks the image (ii. 34) signifying that God,
through His chosen people, λικμήσει πάσας τὰς βασιλείας
(44). The recurrence of the verb λικμᾶν in Lk. xx. 18
indicates that Luke has equated the stone which the
builders rejected of Ps. cxviii. 22, and the stone of stumbling of Is. viii. 14, with the stone of Dan. ii. 34. But this
probably belongs to a later stage of reflection rather than
to the primitive scheme of *testimonia*. Dan. ii does not
otherwise figure in the New Testament.

[1] In the version of Theodotion. The translation of Daniel known to
New Testament writers appears generally to be similar to this version
rather than to the LXX.

[2] I have argued elsewhere (*Parables of the Kingdom*, 3rd Ed., pp. 44-
45) that ἤγγικεν and ἔφθασεν might well be variant translations of the
Aramaic מטא which is used here in Daniel.

Another characteristic Danielic figure taken up in the New Testament, is that of the "abomination of desolation," which is expressly ascribed to "Daniel the prophet" in Mt. xxiv. 15. It occurs in Dan. ix. 27 (according to the Greek versions), xi. 31, xii. 11. It is the last of these which gives signs of occurring in a context which early Christian thinkers regarded as a source of *testimonia*.[1] The following places in Chapter xii appear to be echoed or alluded to:

xii. 1, the great tribulation; cf. Mk. xiii. 19, fairly close verbally.

xii. 2, the resurrection of the dead (here alone, explicitly, in the Old Testament), followed, in sense though not verbally, in Mt. xxv. 46, Jn. v. 28-29.

xii. 5, the righteous λάμψουσιν, echoed in Mt. xiii. 43.

xii. 9, a limit to the time of Gentile oppression, followed in sense, and with some echoes of language, in Lk. xxi. 24.

xii. 12, μακάριος ὁ ὑπομένων; cf. Jas. i. 12, Mk. xiii. 13.[2]

xii. 13, εἰς συντέλειαν ἡμερῶν (closing words of the book); cf. Mt. xxviii. 20 (closing words of the gospel).

It seems highly probable, therefore, that Dan. vii and xii are to be added to the list of scriptures which were early selected as sources of *testimonia*.

In addition to these portions of Joel, Zechariah and Daniel, there are two isolated passages of Malachi which are taken up in the New Testament. The first is iii. 1-6 which speaks of the coming judgment. Verse 1, "Behold, I

[1] Dan. xi. 41 (LXX) might seem to be echoed in Mt. xxiv. 10, σκανδαλισθήσονται πολλοί, but the whole context is alien.

[2] In all three passages it is not endurance in general that is praised, but endurance of the πειρασμός which the servants of God must pass through before the day of salvation.

send out my messenger, and he will prepare a way before my face," is cited in a variant form—varying chiefly in substituting "thy face" for "my face"—in Mt. xi. 10 and Lk. vii. 27, under the rubric γέγραπται. In Mk. i. 2 (in the same version, substantially) it is associated with Is. xl. 3, under the rubric "it is written in Isaiah the prophet."

Since this sentence is evidently an important *testimonium*, it is possible that the continuation of the passage, "and the Lord whom you seek will come suddenly into his temple," was in the minds of the evangelists who recorded the coming of Christ into the temple to purge it of evil things and to claim it for the worship of God, as in Malachi the priesthood is cleansed in order that they may offer a righteous sacrifice (iii. 3); but if so, they have not followed the language of the prophecy.

The closing verses of Mal. iv contain the prophecy of the coming of Elijah before the Day of the Lord. In Mk. ix. 11-12 there is a clear allusion to this prophecy but curiously enough it is introduced not as a reference to scripture, but to what "the scribes say." In Lk. i. 17 there is a clear allusion to the same passage, where it is said that John the Baptist will come "in the spirit and power of Elijah, to turn the hearts of the fathers to the children" (ἐπιστρέψαι is perhaps closer to the meaning of the Hebrew than the ἀποκαθιστάναι of the LXX and Mark), but not, explicitly, that John *is* Elijah.

Whatever may have been the intention of the prophet, for the evangelists the "messenger" of Mal. iii. 1 and the "Elijah" of iv. 5 are identical. All three Synoptics more or less explicitly identify the composite figure with John the Baptist, whom they also identify with the "voice crying in the wilderness" of Isaiah xl. 3. The Fourth Evangelist however, rejects this identification: he makes the Baptist

deny that he is "Elijah," and affirm that he is the "voice"
(Jn. i. 21-23). It seems that there was some difference of
opinion in the early Church. It is possible that the references to Elijah are not part of the primitive body of
testimonies, but the product of early speculation and
controversy upon the status of the Baptist in the context
of current Jewish belief; conceivably that might be why
Mark speaks of a scribal tradition rather than of scripture
as authority for the coming of Elijah. In any case, there
does not seem to be sufficient ground for placing Malachi
among the primary body of scriptures which supplied
testimonies. Most of the book is alien from the New Testament; at most the two short paragraphs, iii. 1-6, iv. 4-5
were utilized, and primarily, it may be, in explication of
the Isaianic prophecy of the "voice," as Mk. i. 2 would
suggest.[1]

The scriptures we have so far reviewed have all the
same general "plot," with manifold variations. They
describe that supreme crisis of history which Joel, like
other prophets, calls the Day of the Lord. It is the intervention of God in history to achieve His purpose for His
creation. This intervention takes the form of judgment
upon the evil things in history, and the establishment of
a people of God, through whom all nations will come under
His everlasting and beneficent reign. The employment of
these scriptures as testimonies to the *kerygma* indicates
that the crisis out of which the Christian movement arose
is regarded as the realization of the prophetic vision of
judgment and redemption. The passages to which reference is made are in general couched in the symbolic

[1] Much as Is. xxviii. 16, from a context which is not itself taken up,
appears chiefly in explication of Is. viii. 14.

language characteristic of apocalyptic literature. We should do less than justice to their authors, and certainly to the New Testament writers who quote them, if we insisted on the kind of crudely literal understanding to which our western minds are prone. Exactly where the attempt at literal description ends and symbolism begins, the writers themselves probably did not know, and we can hardly guess. But we shall be wise to treat the entire scheme of imagery as language appropriate to describe that which lies upon the frontier of normal experience, which therefore cannot be directly communicated in plain speech. But the prophets seriously believed that what they spoke of (in however cryptic terms) would happen. The early Christians believed it had happened, or at least was in process of happening.

There is indeed some ambiguity about the precise stage which the eschatological process has reached at the time when the New Testament documents were written. If we have Joel before us, it is clear that we have got at least as far as the outpouring of the Spirit before the great and terrible Day of the Lord. The moment has come when men invoke the name of the Lord and are saved. The people is being gathered together, the *ecclesia* has been sanctified, and presbyters are being elected. The harvest, according to some places in the New Testament, has already come, and the sickle is at work; in other places the harvest is still pending; the gathering of all nations for final judgment is thought of as future.

If we follow Zechariah, the King has already ridden into Zion, the Shepherd has been slain, the blood of the covenant has been shed, and Israel have looked upon Him whom they pierced—at least according to the Fourth Gospel, though according to the Apocalypse of John that is something yet to come. The temple has been claimed for the nations, and the traders excluded from it; and the gathering of the nations to worship the Lord in holiness is well under way, in the Gentile mission. Yet the coming of the Lord "with all His saints" still tarries.

If we take the visions of Daniel, the coming of the Son of Man "with the clouds" is thought of as future, though in another aspect the Son of Man has come, and in Mt. xxvi. 64 (ἀπ’ ἄρτι) and Lk. xxii. 69 (ἀπὸ τοῦ νῦν) the coming with the clouds is in some sort beginning, and in each of these cases it is coupled with the prophecy of the Lord at God's right hand which the *kerygma* uniformly declares to be already fulfilled.

If Malachi belongs here, we must say that the "messenger," who is Elijah, who is John the Baptist, has (according to the prevailing view) already come, and, perhaps, that the Lord has come to His temple and cleansed it.

The mind of the early Church betrays no uneasiness about these apparent inconsistencies. It felt no difficulty if it had to accept the prophecies as declaring that which had happened, was happening, and would happen, indistinguishably. The tension, in fact, between realization and unfulfilled expectation is thoroughly characteristic of the early Christian outlook, for which the Fourth Evangelist found the appropriate expression: "the moment is coming and is here," ἔρχεται ὥρα καὶ νῦν ἐστίν.

II. *Scriptures of the New Israel*

Under this head we have to consider certain prophecies of Hosea, Isaiah and Jeremiah. In purport they do not greatly differ from the scriptures we have already considered, but they are less deeply coloured by apocalyptic imagery, and approach more nearly to direct description in recognizably historical terms.

In Hosea our starting point is Paul's citation in Rom.
ix. 25-26 (introduced by the words, "as he says in Hosea").
Here the apostle has conflated Hos. ii. 23 and i. 10 in that
order, the former following the LXX fairly closely, the
latter quoted more freely. In I Pet. ii. 10 we have a very
clear reminiscence of the same prophecy, without direct
quotation. It is clearly not based upon the citation in
Romans, for, whereas in Romans the key-words are
λαός and ἀγαπᾶσθαι (after the LXX of ii. 23), in I Peter
the key-words are λαός and ἐλεεῖσθαι (after the LXX of
i. 6-8, ii. 1).[1] The independence of the two authors seems
certain. Both must have followed a pre-canonical tradition
which recognized this prophecy of Hosea as a *testimonium*.
But since their citations oblige us to refer to several
different verses in chapters i and ii, we cannot plausibly
isolate any one single verse as a "proof-text." It appears
that early Christian thinkers had in mind the whole
episode of Lo-ammi and Lo-ruhamah as it is developed in
chapters i-ii, and understood it as a description of the way
in which God, of His sheer grace, adopted as His people
those who formerly were no people of His—for Hosea,
repentant Israel, for Christian teachers, the Gentiles, now
admitted to the true *ecclesia*.

In the rest of the Book of Hosea we can recognize
scattered allusions, but it is not so easy to establish the
use of whole contexts. Hos. xi. 1, "I called my son out of
Egypt," not after the LXX, but in a version closer to the
Hebrew, is quoted in Mt. ii. 15, under the rubric, τό
ῥηθὲν ὑπό κυρίου διὰ τοῦ προφήτου. The citation here
does not appear to have much relation to the immediate
context, but I shall presently try to show that it is not
so completely arbitrary as is sometimes supposed.

[1] The difference is in the LXX, not in the Hebrew, which has רחמה
all through.

There is a clear allusion to Hos. xiii. 14, "O Death, where is thy judgment? O Hades, where is thy sting?" in I Cor. xv. 55, where it is conflated with Is. xxv. 8; and there are suggestions that Hosea xiii may have had an influence on the formation of the tradition which lies behind the "apocalyptic discourse" in the Synoptic Gospels. It is concerned with terrible judgments to fall upon Israel, which are described as ὠδῖνες, and Mk. xiii. 8 uses the same term of the impending troubles, while Lk. xxi. 22 speaks after Hos. ix. 7, of "days of vengeance." In Hos. xiii. 16 these troubles are to fall with especial force upon nursing mothers and pregnant women, again as in Mk. xiii. 17, though Hosea is more particular in describing how the sucking children will be "dashed to the ground" (ἐδαφισθήσονται). This trait is added by Luke in a kindred passage, xix. 44. Although, therefore, we cannot recognize any specific *testimonia* in this context, it seems more than possible that Hosea xiii is a significant part of the background of early Christian thought, and that when Paul used the magnificent apostrophe "Death, where is thy sting?" as the climax of his prophetic affirmation of the resurrection of the dead, he was not employing a casual literary reminiscence, but referring to a passage already recognized as a classical description of God's deliverance of His people out of utter destruction.

If this be accepted, we may consider another passage which similarly speaks of judgment and deliverance, Hos. v. 8 – vi. 3.[1] It begins with the now familiar trumpet-call, and the command, "proclaim" (κηρύξατε). Then follows a severe condemnation of Israel's rebellion, and

---

[1] Some modern critics, for reasons which do not appear to me particularly cogent, prefer to treat vi. 1-3 as ironical. Whether or not this be so, we are not to suppose that any early Christian suspected it. He would naturally take it at its face value.

sentence upon them. This leads on to an act of repentance and return to God. The prophet puts into the mouth of the people the comforting reflection, "After two days he will revive us: on the third day he will raise us up and we shall live before him. And let us know, let us follow on to know the Lord." In the LXX this runs, ". . . on the third day we shall both rise, and live before him, and know: we shall press on to know the Lord." Although this passage is never expressly quoted in the New Testament, it seems to be echoed in the clause which Paul cites from the primitive *kerygma:* "He was raised on the third day according to the scriptures." Indeed it seems impossible to find any other scripture which speaks of rising (or being raised) on the third day, and there is a fairly wide consensus to accept Hos. vi. 3 as the place which Paul (or more properly those from whom he received the tradition) intended. That its employment as a testimony to the resurrection of Christ is not so arbitrary or unreasonable as might appear, I shall try to show presently.

In the same chapter there is a verse (6) which is cited in Mt. ix. 13 and xii. 7: "I desire mercy and not sacrifice," but the evangelist does not seem to have taken any particular account of the context.

In addition to the passages already mentioned, we find sporadically through the book expressions which, to say the least, would be congenial to any early Christian "searching the scriptures" for light upon the *kerygma* or the gospel facts: the references to God's "covenant" with His people (ii. 18, x. 4), the affirmation of their "redemption" (vii. 13, xiii. 14), Israel as a "vine" (x. 1), and, we may add, the frequent references to the "knowledge" of God as the mark of the renewed Israel, which is Christ's gift to His people in Mt. xi. 27 (= Lk. x. 22), in the Pauline Epistles and frequently in John.

F

I believe we are justified in concluding that the whole of this short book of Hosea was influential in early Christian thought, while chapters i-ii and perhaps xiii and v. 8 – vi. 3 had especial significance. These passages bring into clear relief what is a dominant theme all through: the theme of judgment upon a sinful people as the inevitable and indispensable, but also the certain, prelude to redemption, renewal, or resurrection.

In the Book of Isaiah we find a starting point in the prophecy of the "hardening" of Israel in vi. 9-10, repeatedly cited or echoed by New Testament writers, to whom it appears to have been known in at least two Greek versions (see pp. 36-39). John, as we have seen, refers to the context in which the prophecy appears—Isaiah's vision of the glory of the Lord. The hymn of the seraphim in vi. 3 must early have passed into Christian liturgical use, for it appears already in Rev. iv. 8. We need therefore have no hesitation in setting down the whole of chapter vi as a scripture to which the early Church readily turned for testimony, inspiration, and instruction.

In chapter viii, again, we have the important primitive *testimonium* about the stone of stumbling and rock of offence (viii. 14), which was early conjoined with the prophecy of the foundation stone of Zion in Is. xxviii. 16 (see pp. 41-43). But this is not the only place in this chapter to which early Christian thinkers gave attention. Consider the following:

viii. 12-13, "Fear not their fear . . . etc.," quoted in
 1 Pet. iii. 14-15.

viii. 17, "I will trust in him," quoted in Heb. ii. 13 (under the rubric λέγων).

viii. 18, "Behold, I and the children whom God has given me," quoted (under the rubric λέγων) in Heb. ii. 13 (see p. 20).

viii. 22, θλῖψις καὶ στενοχωρία, taken up in Rom. ii. 9.

Further, in viii. 8, 10, we have the watchword עִמָּנוּאֵל, which the LXX here renders μεθ' ἡμῶν ὁ θεός. The prophet is here referring back to the "sign" of Immanuel in vii. 14, where the LXX transliterates without translating. This prophecy is quoted in full in Mt. i. 23 under the rubric, τὸ ῥηθὲν ὑπὸ κυρίου διὰ τοῦ προφήτου. The LXX is followed closely, except for two minor verbal changes, with the transliterated Ἐμμανουήλ, to which the evangelist then adds the translation, μεθ' ἡμῶν ὁ θεός, from the LXX of viii. 8, 10. His interest in the idea of "God-with-us" is probably to be traced also in the closing verse of this gospel, where ἐγὼ μεθ' ὑμῶν takes the place of μεθ' ἡμῶν ὁ θεός—appropriately enough, since the Lord who is to be with His Church perpetually is "Immanuel" in the full sense.

But interest in this idea is not confined to the first gospel. The phrase of Isaiah is echoed in Rev. xxi. 3,[1] in a passage which describes "the holy city, New Jerusalem," and so might form a fit counterpart to the prophecy of mingled promise and threat addressed to the old Jerusalem of Ahaz, which provides the original setting for the "sign" of Immanuel. It would therefore be unsafe to assume that the exploitation of the Immanuel prophecy as a testimony was confined to the first evangelist.

[1] This echo is present, whatever reading we adopt among the variants. I owe to Dr. Austin Farrer the attractive suggestion that if we adopt the reading of A and some other authorities, the words ὁ θεὸς μετ' αὐτῶν should be understood as a title, equivalent to "Immanuel," and we should render, "God-with-them shall be their God."

In Is. vii. 3 the name Shear-jashub, meaning "A remnant will turn," is the first introduction of an idea which plays a significant part in subsequent chapters of Isaiah, and is exploited by Paul, who cites Is. x. 22-23 (Rom. ix. 27-28) and i. 9 (Rom. 29), but not, apparently, vii. 3, where the LXX renders ὁ καταλειφθεὶς Ἰασούβ. It would therefore be precarious to infer that he had chapter vii in mind. On the other hand, in view of the importance of chapter vii as the original setting of the "Immanuel" idea, it remains possible that this chapter, lying between chapters vi and viii, both of which are important sources of *testimonia*, may have belonged to a continuous block of scripture early studied for this purpose: I believe it is in fact probable.

Returning to chapter viii, and going forward, we observe that ix. 1-2 is quoted, under the rubric τὸ ῥηθὲν διὰ Ἡσαΐου τοῦ προφήτου, in Mt. iv. 15-16, in a version differing from the LXX, and in some respects nearer to the Hebrew. Before concluding that this is one of the *testimonia* which we owe exclusively to the biblical learning of the first evangelist, we must note that the clause of the *Benedictus*, "dawn from the height to give light to those who sit in darkness and the shadow of death" (Lk. i. 79) clearly echoes Is. ix. 2.[1] Further, Matthew cites the prophecy as being fulfilled in the fact that Jesus began His ministry in Galilee; but Jn. ii. 11 similarly calls attention to the fact that the *beginning* of the manifestation of the glory of the Lord was in Galilee.[2] This emphasis

[1] Luke's ἀνατολή, echoing Matthew's ἀνέτειλεν, might suggest that both go back to a common non-septuagintal version of Is. ix. 1-2.

[2] I have elsewhere mentioned a suggestion which I owe to Mr. Hugh Montefiore, that the "beginning of signs" in Galilee, which takes the form of the provision of drink for the thirsty, may be not altogether unconnected with the phrase of the LXX in this place, τοῦτο πρῶτον πίε.

on the beginning in Galilee seems to have been integral to the pattern of the *kerygma* from the first.[1]

The verses thus cited by Matthew are in Isaiah the proem of a prophecy which may properly be called "messianic," since it forecasts a victorious ruler of the dynasty of David who will reign perpetually in righteousness. This prophecy however is never quoted in the New Testament, and allusions are scanty and vague. Lk. i. 32-33 echoes Is. ix. 7 (with a glance also at II Sam. vii. 13, 16, and Dan. vii. 14). The cheers of the crowd for "the coming kingdom of our father David" in Mk. xi. 10 may be a further reminiscence. We might have expected that the birth of the child in ix. 6, and his titles, and especially the announcement of his peaceful reign, would have afforded testimonies; but it is not so. The most we can say is that some traits of the child born to be king in this passage have entered into the generalized picture of the Messiah Son of David which is presupposed in the development of early Christian thought, though it is not its dominant strain.[2] In this sense only we may include ix. 1-7 among the scriptures which afforded primitive testimonies. The rest of chapter ix is alien.

If we now look back, it will appear that there is some ground for believing that Is. vi. 1 – ix. 7 may have formed, for early Christian students of the Old Testament, a single complex unit of prophecy. Beginning with a vision of the glory of God, it first pronounces the doom of

[1] See Acts x. 38, in a form of *kerygma* which more than any other appears to correspond to the pattern underlying the structure of Mark. It is not insignificant that this element of the *kerygma* persisted so strongly in face of the tendency to canonize Jerusalem as the place of origin of the Christian mission; see Lk. xxiv. 47, Acts i. 8, and perhaps even Rom. xv. 19.

[2] It contended with a certain distaste for the whole conception of the Davidic Messiah; see Mk. xii. 37, Jn. vii. 41-42.

rebellious Israel. There follows a passage in which the judgment is particularized in terms which, while they primarily refer to the perils of the time of Ahaz, a first-century reader might readily interpret in timeless, or contemporary, reference. But embedded in the sombre picture of judgment is the promise of "God with us," which sounds as a watchword through the following chapter; and perhaps also that of the returning Remnant ("Shear-jashub"), which for Paul at least was crucial. In the strength of these promises, God's people are exhorted to have no fear, but to hallow the Lord in their hearts (viii. 12-13), while to the disloyal He will be "a stone of stumbling and a rock of offence" (viii. 14).

The prophet now presents the loyal remnant as "the children whom God has given me" (viii. 18)—whom our first-century reader will understand as the nucleus of the true *ecclesia*, and by no means without some historical warrant. There now ensues a period of "tribulation and dire straits" (viii. 22), which for our supposed first-century reader will readily fall in with the general conception of the great tribulation preceding the Day of the Lord. And so finally the Day dawns, with light for them who sit in darkness and the shadow of death, and the endless reign of the Son of David. If we suppose the early Church to have read this part of Isaiah in some such sense as that, each of the brief extracts which appear as *testimonia* bears a far more intelligible and constructive significance than if they were cited as isolated "proof-texts."

The succeeding chapters of Isaiah yield little to our purpose. As we have seen, the short *pericope* about the Remnant in ix. 27-29 is adduced by Paul in the course of his great argument in Rom. ix-xi (cited, along with Is.

i. 9, in Rom. ix. 27-29), without reference to its immediate
context: its true context is rather in vi-ix, where the boy
Shear-jashub is introduced as a sign.

The "messianic" prophecy of xi. 1-10 has, as might be
expected, found some echoes in the New Testament, which
may be listed as follows:

xi. 2, The Spirit resting on the Messiah, cf. the Gospels
    (John's μένον ἐπ' αὐτόν, i. 33, is the nearest to
    Isaiah's ἀναπαύσεται ἐπ' αὐτόν).
xi. 3, οὐ κατὰ τὴν δόξαν κρινεῖ, remotely echoed in Jn.
    vii. 24.
xi. 10, the Root of Jesse, quoted in full, Rom. xv. 12,
    exactly as in the MS. text of the LXX, under the
    rubric, Ἡσαΐας λέγει. The "Root of David" in Rev.
    v. 5 is probably an inexact reminiscence of the same
    passage.

This is just enough to prove that the *pericope* was among
the scriptures which yielded testimonies; the wonder is
that it did not attract more attention. After this point
there is a long tract of the Book of Isaiah which is barren
for our purpose.

In Is. xxviii, we have already noted the verse about the
foundation stone of Zion (16), which was used in explication of the prophecy of the stone of stumbling in Is.
viii. 14, but does not seem to have been used as a testimony
in its own right, or related to its context. The citation of
xxviii. 11 in I Cor. xiv. 21 (under the rubric "It is written
in the Law," and in a version widely different from the
LXX, and nearer to the Hebrew) seems again quite un-
related to the context, and has no particular significance
for our present purpose.

Is. xxix, however, contains one short pericope, 9-14,
which, as it happens, is cited by Paul and in the Synoptic
Gospels.

xxix. 10, is quoted (under the rubric καθάπερ γέγραπται) in
Rom. xi. 8, where it is conflated with a passage apparently from Deut. xxix. 4, about eyes that do not see
and ears that do not hear. Paul clearly connected it
with the declaration of the hardening of Israel in
vi. 9-10 (cf. p. 38).

xxix. 13, is cited (under the rubric, ἐπροφήτευσεν Ἡσαΐας
. . . ὡς γέγραπται) in Mk. vii. 6-7, Mt. xv. 8-9, in
identical terms, close to the LXX, as also in the
gospel fragment, Pap. Egerton 2.

xxix. 14, "I will destroy the wisdom of the wise . . .", is
cited (under the rubric γέγραπται) in I Cor. i. 19.

There is thus some reason to infer that this *pericope* was
in the early Church brought together with other prophecies
of the contumacy of Israel, which were employed especially
in relation to the argument about the extension of the
Gospel from the Jews to the Gentiles.

But it is only when we come to chapter xl that we reach
again a really important source of testimonies. Here we
have, in xl. 1-11, a *locus classicus* of the hope of redemption. The vocabulary of the passage is such as was peculi-
arly congenial to early Christianity: παρακαλεῖν, σωτήριον,
εὐαγγελίζεσθαι, κύριος ἔρχεται. Over and above this, we
have the following citations or reminiscences:

xl. 1, "the voice of one crying in the wilderness . . .",
quoted Mk. i. 3 (under the rubric γέγραπται ἐν τῷ
Ἡσαΐα τῷ προφήτῃ (cf. pp. 39-41).

xl. 5, ὀφθήσεται ἡ δόξα κυρίου (cf. Jn. xi. 40 ὄψῃ τὴν
δόξαν τοῦ θεοῦ)).

xl. 6-8, "All flesh is grass . . .", quoted in full in I Pet. i. 24-
25, with the significant comment, τοῦτο δέ ἐστίν τὸ
ῥῆμα τὸ εὐαγγελισθὲν εἰς ὑμᾶς.

xl. 11, the Shepherd and His flock; cf. Jn. x. 1-16 (though
this owes more to Ezek. xxxiv, where the image of
the shepherd is greatly elaborated).

Clearly we need have no hesitation in adding this *pericope* to our list of scriptures employed for testimonies. Other passages in the "Deutero-Isaiah" will be more appropriately placed in another group.

To these prophecies of Hosea and Isaiah it seems that we should add at least one passage from Jeremiah. We have already noted the great importance for early Christian thought of the prophecy of the New Covenant in Jer. xxxi. 31-34. There is a further quotation from this chapter in Mt. ii. 18, where (under the rubric τὸ ῥηθὲν διὰ Ἱερεμίου τοῦ προφήτου) the prophecy of "Rachel weeping for her children" (Jer. xxxi. 15) is given in a non-septuagintal version. With this in mind, we observe that the preceding verses are unusually full of ideas and expressions congenial to New Testament writers: e.g., verse 10, the idea of the "gathering" (συνάγειν) of God's people, as in Jn. xi. 52, Mk. xiii. 27, and of Israel as the flock fed by God, as in Jn. x. 9 (the verb βόσκειν as in Jn. xxi. 17); verse 11, the "redemption" (λυτροῦν) of Israel; verse 12, the feeding of the hungry; cf. Lk. vi. 21, Jn. vi. 35, Rev. vii. 16, οὐ πεινάσουσιν ἔτι, as here, though otherwise the quotation follows Is. xlix. 10; verse 14, τῶν ἀγαθῶν μου ἐμπλησθήσεται cf. Jn. vi. 12, ὡς ἐνεπλήσθησαν[1] (and note that in the "Woe" corresponding to the beatitude on the hungry, Lk. vi. 25, the same verb is used, suggesting that it is an alternative for χορτασθῆναι in such contexts). The expression ψυχὴν πεινῶσαν ἐνέπλησα recurs in verse 25, though

[1] I include these references, here and elsewhere, to the gospel narratives of the feeding of the multitude on the hypothesis, which I believe they help to justify, that those narratives are intended to represent it as an "eschatological" event.

apart from this there is little of this quasi-Christian vocabulary between the prophecy of weeping Rachel and the prophecy of the New Covenant. In all this, although there is nothing that could be described as a direct echo of Jeremiah, yet there is perhaps enough affinity of language to suggest that the whole passage is the kind of scripture which had influence on early Christian vocabulary. We may therefore, with some reserve, associate Jer. xxxi. 10-34, which as a whole describes the tribulation and renewal of Israel, with the prophecies of Hosea and Isaiah dealing with the same theme, as a source of testimonies.

It seems possible that we ought further to add Jer. vii. 1-15, a prophecy of the doom of the temple. It is true that only one phrase out of this prophecy recurs in the New Testament, where the temple is described as a "den of thieves" (or more properly, a "brigands' cave"), Mk. xi. 17, in contrast to its true function as defined in Is. lvi. 7, "a house of prayer for all nations." The prophecy speaks of the destruction of the temple at Jerusalem, as the earlier temple at Shiloh had been destroyed, and although there is no echo of language, in substance the forecast of the destruction of the temple in Mk. xiii. 2 is similar. It is possible enough that the allusion to the "den of thieves" was intended to send the hearers back to Jeremiah, where they would find reason enough for the foreboding that the temple was doomed to destruction. This would provide a clue to the somewhat elusive connection, in the Gospels, between the cleansing of the temple and forecasts of its destruction. But the passage scarcely qualifies for inclusion here. At most we may say that the spirit of these prophecies of doom in Jeremiah is recognizable in several passages of the Gospels. (Cf. echoes of the language of Jeremiah in the predictions of the

destruction of Jerusalem, as set forth in my article,
"The Fall of Jerusalem and the Abomination of Desolation," in *Journal of Roman Studies*, Vol. xxxvii (1947).)

With this group of scriptures we must place the passage
of Habakkuk (ii. 3-4) which, as we have seen, is adduced
by Paul and the Author to the Hebrews. In the preceding
chapter we have the single passage, "Behold, ye despisers,
and wonder and perish . . ." (i. 5), which is quoted in
Acts xiii. 41, in a form very close to the LXX, under the
rubric "That which is spoken in the prophets." In its
original context it is a warning of the approaching terrors
of a Chaldæan invasion. As cited in Acts it is a warning of
the divine sentence of rejection upon rebellious Israel as
represented by the Jews who refuse to hear the Gospel.
There are no further echoes of this short book in the New
Testament.[1] The spirit of Hab. i is different from that of
most of the other prophecies we have noticed, in that the
sufferings to fall upon Israel seem to be contemplated less
as a divinely sent judgment upon their iniquities, than as
misfortunes from which they confidently appeal to God
for deliverance. In this respect the prophecy is closer to
some of the Psalms which we shall consider in the next
group. But it seems just possible that for early Christian
readers Hab. i-ii fell into the same general pattern as
Hosea and Is. vi-ix, chapter i depicting Israel under
the divine displeasure, and the short oracle ii. 1-4 an-
nouncing the certainty of deliverance, and that in this
sense it was variously adduced to point to the "determinate counsel of God" carried out in the tragic exclusion

[1] Unless we should include Hab. ii. 16 among the passages of the Old
Testament which underlie the particularly pregnant use of the image of
the "cup" in various passages of the Gospels: cf. also Is. li. 17, 22.

of the Jewish people, in the coming of the Deliverer, and in the salvation of those who put their faith in Christ.

In this whole group of prophecies, then, which speak of the emergence of a new Israel after terrible judgments, we have a body of scripture which can be shown with a high degree of probability to have been employed by early Christian teachers in elucidating the themes of the *kerygma*. The whole process of judgment and renewal is conceived as "fulfilled" in the Gospel facts. If we ask, as before, at what point in the process the early Christian observer supposed himself to be standing, the answer is less equivocal than it was in regard to our first group. The "hardening" of Israel, the "stone of stumbling," and in general the judgment of God upon His disloyal people, are conceived as already within the experience of those who witnessed the events of the life and death of Jesus; and equally the calling of the "remnant," the inauguration of the New Covenant, the designation of "Lo-ammi" as "Ammi" and the abiding presence of "God with us" (Immanuel) are conceived as realized in the emergence of the Church, which thus figures as the new (and true) Israel of God, revealed through a process of πτῶσις καὶ ἀνάστασις (Lk. ii. 34). The coming of Christ is the moment at which judgment is passed on decadent Israel and the new people of God comes into being.

III. *Scriptures of the Servant of the Lord and the Righteous Sufferer*

Under this head I shall place certain passages in the latter part of the Book of Isaiah, together with a group of psalms which seem to have a certain affinity with them.

Our starting point is the citation of Is. xlii. 1-4 in Mt. xii. 18-21. The passage in its original context introduces for the first time the figure of the Servant of the Lord. Matthew cites it under the rubric "That which was spoken through Isaiah the prophet," with an obvious sense of its importance as pointing to the "determinate counsel of God" which was fulfilled in the programme of the ministry of Jesus. The quotation does not follow the LXX; indeed, at almost every point where it is possible to substitute a different verb or noun, the substitution is made. Where the LXX most markedly differs from the Massoretic text, in giving to the Servant the names Jacob and Israel (verse 1), Matthew's version is much closer to the Hebrew. It seems clear that we have here an alternative, non-septuagintal version of the passage.[1] It is noteworthy that where the LXX renders בְּחִירִי רָצְתָה נַפְשִׁי by ὁ ἐκλεκτός μου, προσεδέξατο αὐτὸν ἡ ψυχή μου, Matthew has ὁ ἀγαπητός μου ὃν εὐδόκησεν ἡ ψυχή μου. It seems that we are to recognize the same rendering of Is. xlii. 1 behind the form of the *bath-qol* at the baptism of Jesus, as we have it in Mk. i. 11, or, more nearly still, in Mt. iii. 17: at the moment when the Spirit rests upon Him, the divine voice declares Him to be ὁ ἀγαπητὸς ἐν ᾧ εὐδόκησα. The intention to identify Jesus with the Servant of the Lord announced in Is. xlii could hardly be made clearer.

In what immediately follows there is no further passage which is expressly quoted, and this writer's manner of letting his thought play about a few key-concepts which constantly recur makes it difficult to identify particular sentences which may have been in the mind of New

[1] On the other hand, Lk. i. 54, ἀντελάβετο Ἰσραὴλ παιδὸς αὐτοῦ, appears to be a reminiscence of the LXX of Is. xlii. 1 (cf. also xli. 8-9, LXX).

Testament writers who are obviously working with the same concepts. But it may be worth while to draw attention to the following places in xlii-xliv. 5:

xlii. 6, διαθήκη, *passim* in New Testament.

xlii. 7, sight for the blind, liberty for captives, light for those who "sit in darkness"; cf. Mt. xi. 5, Lk. i. 79, &c.

xlii. 12, the ἀρεταί of God; cf. I Pet. ii. 9; but see also Is. xliii. 21.

xlii. 16, light for darkness, again, *passim*.

xlii. 18, the blind see, the deaf hear; cf. Gospels *passim*.

xliii. 1, "redemption," *passim* in New Testament.

xliii. 2, 5, "I am with thee" (*quasi* "Immanuel") cf. Mt. xxviii. 20.

xliii. 7, "all who invoke my name"; see p. 47.

xliii. 10, "be my witnesses"; cf. Acts i. 8, v. 32, Jn. xv. 26-27[1] (in the two latter places note that "you and the Spirit" replaces "you, and I the Lord, and my Servant").

xliii. 18, "I make new things," quoted Rev. xxi. 5, cf. II Cor. v. 17-18.

xliii. 21, λαόν μου ὃν περιεποιησάμην τὰς ἀρετάς μου διηγεῖσθαι; cf. I Pet. ii. 9, λαὸς εἰς περιποίησιν ὅπως τὰς ἀρετὰς ἐξαγγείλητε τοῦ . . . καλέσαντος.

xliv. 1-2, my servant, my beloved, my chosen; cf. Mk. i. 11, etc.

xliv. 3, water for the thirsty; cf. Jn. iv. 12-14.

xliv. 3, gift of the Spirit, *passim* in New Testament.

From this point on echoes become both vaguer and far fewer. It appears as if Is. xlii. 1 – xliv. 5 formed a compact body of scripture about the Servant which had wide influence on early Christian thought.

[1] The curious affinity between Jn. xv. 26-27 and Acts v. 32 suggests that at a stage much earlier than the developed Johannine theology the "witness" of God through His Servant had been the subject of reflection in the early Church.

In chapters xlix-li we have a further group of passages echoed in the New Testament, though it is not so clear that they belong to a continuous body of scripture. It is noteworthy that in xlix. 3, 5, we have δοῦλος for παῖς, and this term, as we shall see, recurs in a Pauline passage where the Isaianic idea of the Servant is in view. The following places are worth considering:

xlix. 3, God "glorified" in the Servant; cf. Jn. xiii. 31, xvii. 1, Phil. ii. 7, 11.

xlix. 5, the "gathering" of God's people through the Servant; cf. Jn. xi. 52, Mk. xiii. 27.

xlix. 6, "covenant of the people, light of the Gentiles," Acts xiii. 47, with xlix. 8, "covenant of the Gentiles," cf. Lk. ii. 31, &c.

xlix. 9, τοῖς ἐν τῷ σκότει ἀνακαλυφθῆναι; cf. Lk. ii. 32, φῶς εἰς ἀποκάλυψιν.

xlix. 10, "they shall hunger no more . . ." quoted Rev. vii. 16.

l. 6, "I gave my back to smiters (LXX, εἰς μάστιγας), and my cheeks to blows (LXX, τὰς σιαγόνας εἰς ῥαπίσματα), and I did not turn my face away from the shame of spittings (ἐμπτυσμάτων)." This verse is echoed in descriptions of the sufferings of Christ, Mk. xiv. 65 (ἐμπτύειν, ῥαπίσμασιν), Mt. xxvi. 67 (ἐνέπτυσαν εἰς τὸ πρόσωπον, ἐράπισαν), Mk. xv. 15, Mt. xxvii. 26 (φραγελλωσας), Jn. xviii. 22 (ῥάπισμα), xix. 3 (ῥαπίσματα).

l. 7 (LXX), ἔθηκα τὸ πρόσωπόν μου ὡς στερεὰν πέτραν, cf. Lk. ix. 51, τὸ πρόσωπον ἐστήρισεν.

l. 8, ἐγγίζει ὁ δικαιώσας με τίς ὁ κρινόμενός με; cf. Rom. viii. 33.

l. 10 (LXX), οἱ πορευόμενοι ἐν σκότει καὶ οὐκ ἔστιν αὐτοῖς φῶς, cf. Jn. xii. 35, &c.

li. 4-5, recurs to the ideas and expressions of xlix. 6, but apart from this, possible echoes in li and in lii down to verse 12 are vague and scanty.

It appears then that at least xlix. 1-13 and l. 4-11 constituted units of scripture which were recognized as a source of *testimonia*. The intervening passages do not appear for the most part closely related to New Testament language and ideas. Yet xlix. 24-25 unexpectedly finds an echo in Mk. iii. 27. The LXX yields the following meaning: "Shall one take spoils from a giant? . . . Thus saith the Lord, If one takes a giant prisoner, he will take his spoils, and taking them from the strong he shall be saved." There is no verbal resemblance in Mark to the Greek of the LXX, but the sense is so similar that it is difficult to suppose the similarity is accidental. We should perhaps infer that the LXX and the Greek version in Mark both represent, independently, a common tradition of the meaning of the passage, although it is not the natural meaning of the Massoretic text.

The next cluster of passages quoted or echoed in the New Testament occur in the poem of the Suffering Servant in Is. lii. 13 – liii. 12. They may be set forth as follows:

lii. 13 (LXX), ὁ παῖς μου . . . ὑψωθήσεται καὶ δοξασθήσεται, cf. Acts iii. 13, ἐδόξασεν τὸν παῖδα αὐτοῦ, (ii. 33, v. 31, ὑψοῦν), Jn. xii. 23 (δοξάζειν[1]), 32 (ὑψοῦν) *et passim*: Php. ii. 9 (of the δοῦλος), ὑπερύψωσεν.

lii. 15 (LXX), "They shall see to whom it had not been reported concerning him, and they shall understand who had not heard," quoted (with slight differences in order of words) in Rom. xv. 21, under rubric γέγραπται.

liii. 1 (LXX), "Who believed . . . ?", quoted Rom. x. 16, Jn. xii. 38 (see p. 39).

liii. 3, "despised and rejected";[2] cf. Mk. ix. 12 (non-septuagintal, but cf. LXX of Ps. xxii. 6).

[1] The subject here is the "Son of Man," a title which the New Testament writers evidently regarded as interchangeable with "Servant."

[2] The LXX here departs widely from the Massoretic text, but the

liii. 4, "bore our griefs and carried our sorrows," quoted, under rubric τὸ ῥηθὲν διὰ Ἡσαΐου τοῦ προφήτου, in Mt. viii. 17, in non-septuagintal version.

liii. 5, "with his stripes we are healed," I Pet. ii. 24 (moulded on LXX).

liii. 6, "sheep gone astray," I Pet. ii. 25 (following LXX freely).

liii. 7-8a (LXX), "he is led as a sheep . . ." quoted in Acts viii. 32-33, as a περιοχὴ τῆς γραφῆς from "the prophet Isaiah."

liii. 9, "no guile in his mouth" (freely after LXX), I Pet. ii. 22.

liii. 10, "an offering for sin" (περὶ ἁμαρτίας); cf. Rom. viii. 3. The LXX rendering of אָשָׁם is adopted, but the sense of the Massoretic text is retained, the LXX having departed widely from it.

liii. 11, "himself bore our sins" (freely after LXX), I Pet. ii. 24.

liii. 11-12, the repeated, and peculiar "many" (only partly represented in LXX) seems to underly Mk. x. 45, xiv. 24.

liii. 12, "divide the spoil with the strong"; cf. Lk. xi. 21-22, τὰ σκῦλα διαδίδωσιν, with LXX μεριεῖ τὰ σκῦλα.

liii. 12 (LXX), "numbered with the transgressors," quoted Lk. xxii. 37 (with slight verbal change), under rubric τὸ γεγραμμένον.

liii. 12 (LXX), "delivered for our iniquities"; cf. Rom. iv. 25.

liii. 12, "poured out his soul unto death"; cf. Phil. ii. 7-8, ἑαυτὸν ἐκένωσεν . . . . μέχρι θανάτου (the verb ערה, here rendered in LXX παρεδόθη, is elsewhere rendered by ἐκκενοῦν (see J. T. S. xxxix. (1938), p. 292).

root בזה recurs in Ps. xxii. 6, where it is represented by ἐξουδένημα. Accordingly, the נִבְזֶה of Is. liii. 3 would be properly rendered by ἐξουδενήθη. Mark therefore is correctly representing this prophecy when he says γέγραπται ἵνα ἐξουδενηθῇ. Once again "Son of Man" takes the place of "Servant."

liii. 12 (LXX), "bore the sins of many," Heb. ix. 28.

liii. 12, "made intercession" (non-septuagintal); cf. Rom. viii. 34.

Here then we have a long, self-contained passage, practically every verse of which is represented in one way or another in the New Testament, and in almost every part of it—Synoptic Gospels, John, Acts, Paul, Hebrews and I Peter. Its importance as a source of *testimonia* is manifest, and there is a high probability, in view of its ubiquity, that its use as such goes back to the earliest period to which we have access.

With the scriptures of the Servant of the Lord we must associate Is. lxi. 1-2, which is quoted as the programme of the ministry of Jesus in Lk. iv. 18-19, and echoed in Acts x. 38, Mt. xi. 5 = Lk. vii. 22, Mt. v. 4 (see pp. 52-53). It is true that the person here described is not given the title "Servant," but his functions are so like those of the Servant in chapter xlii that the identification is easily made—and is in fact not far astray. It does not appear that the rest of this chapter was laid under contribution for testimonies, but the ideas of the priestly people in verse 6 (cf. I Pet. ii. 9, Rev. i. 6), of the "eternal covenant" in verse 8, and of the people of God as a bride in verse 10 (cf. Rev. xxi. 2, 9, II Cor. xi. 2, Eph. v. 25-27) are all in one way or another directly related to the central *rôle* of Christ. We may therefore with probability include this chapter among the scriptures determinative of the early Christian understanding of the Gospel. But undoubtedly the chief importance of the passage lay in the fact that it enabled the Church to answer the question, In what sense was Jesus "anointed" ("Messiah")? Granted that He is to be recognized as the Servant spoken of in Is. xlii &c., and that it is as such that He is endowed with the Spirit, for specific functions amply illustrated in

the relevant scriptures, then Is. lxi. 1-2 justifies the conclusion that this endowment with the Spirit is in fact His
"anointing" (for the same functions). It is clearly this line
of thought that lies behind the formulation "God anointed
him with holy Spirit" in Acts x. 38.

As we noted above, Luke has (inadvertently, no doubt)
interpolated into the quotation of Is. lxi. 1-2 a clause from
Is. lviii. 6, and the occurrence in juxtaposition of several
ideas congenial to early Christian thought in lviii. 6-10
perhaps justifies the inclusion of this passage as a supple-
mentary item. In chapter lx also we have the collocation
of the ideas of light, the glory of the Lord, the gathering
of Israel, and the description of the holy city in verse 11
which is quoted in Rev. xxi. 25-26. But there is scarcely
sufficient evidence to allow us to include this chapter
among the primary scriptural authorities for the interpretation of the *kerygma*.

For our present purpose it is fortunately not necessary
to decide the much-debated question whether the Servant
was conceived originally as an individual figure or as a
personification of a collectivity.[1] What is clear is that in
the text of Isaiah as it has come down to us there is an
alternation between the corporate connotation, where the
Servant is equated with "Israel," or "Jacob," and the
individual, where he is a quasi-prophetic figure with a
mission to Israel. There seems to be at present less unani-
mity among critics than formerly appeared, in solving the
problem by the hypothesis of difference of authorship,

[1] Writers of the Scandinavian school now tend to find in the Servant
traits of the ancient ritual myth of the divine king, which (if the theory
were to find general acceptance) would bring this figure into an aborigi-
nal relation to other concepts with which it is associated in early Christian thought. But it would not alter the fact that in the text of II Isaiah
as we have it the individual and the corporate elements in the idea
are alternative or intermingled.

and it is not impossible that the alternation of meaning is integral to the conception. In the New Testament there is only one place where the Servant is unambiguously identified with Israel, Lk. i. 54. Elsewhere, even passages in which the original distinctly equates the Servant with Israel are directly applied to Christ (e.g. xlix. 3). Yet there are evidences that the corporate, or representative, character of the Servant-figure is not entirely out of view. Thus xliv. 1-2, which most emphatically declares Israel to be the Servant, is echoed in passages of the New Testament where his attributes, "the beloved," "the chosen" are given to Christ; yet the promise of water to the thirsty (verse 3) is confirmed not to Christ but to His people, as the Spirit, even in the original, is promised to the "seed" of the Servant, and as in xliii. 1-5, xliv. 21-24 the assurances "I have redeemed thee," and "I am with thee," are made to Israel, the Servant, and fulfilled to the Church.

There is a certain parallelism here with the treatment of the "Son of Man" figure, which is in Daniel vii declared to be a personification of "the people of the saints of the Most High," but in the New Testament is applied as a title of Christ, yet frequently in contexts where the collective or corporate aspects of the figure are clearly in view. We shall be confronted with similar phenomena in our next group of scriptures, taken from the Psalter.

We may conveniently start our consideration of the psalms in question with Ps. lxix, where we found that one half of verse 22 was quoted by Paul and the other half by John, while other verses are quoted or recalled in Mark, Matthew, John and Acts, the almost irresistible conclusion being that the authors of all these works were aware of the psalm in its entirety as a source of *testimonia* (see pp.

57-59). The psalmist appeals to God out of a situation of dire distress. He describes his sufferings, which are endured in God's cause, and the malice of his enemies, prays for their overthrow and for his own deliverance, and ends with thankful praises to God for the certainty of salvation. Through most of the poem we should suppose the writer to be speaking of his individual lot, but from time to time it is evident that he represents a larger unity, and in the end it is the salvation of Zion which is acclaimed. The intention of New Testament writers is clearly to apply the whole to the sufferings and ultimate triumph of Christ.

Psalm xxii is similar in purport, and a whole series of its expressions are quoted or echoed in the New Testament:

xxii. 1, "... *lema sabachthani?*", Mk. xv. 34, Mt. xxvii. 46.
xxii. 6, "despised of the people," cf. Is. liii. 3, Mk. ix. 12.
xxii. 7, ἐξεμυκτήρισαν, Lk. xxiii. 35.
   ἐκίνησαν κεφαλήν, Mk. xv. 29.
xxii. 8, "let him deliver him," Mt. xxvii. 43.
xxii. 18, "they parted my garments ... " quoted as γραφή
  Jn. xix. 24; cf. Mk. xv. 24.
xxii. 20, μονογενής Jn. i. 18.
xxii. 22, "I will declare thy name ..." quoted Heb. ii. 12.
xxii. 24, "when he cried unto him he heard"; cf. Heb. v. 7.
xxii. 27, "the meek shall eat and be satisfied"; cf. Lk.
  vi. 20-21.
xxii. 28, "the kingdom is the Lord's"; Rev. xi. 15 (cf.
  Mt. vi. 13 in T.R., representing liturgical usage).

All these seem to be fairly clear and direct. Less clear and direct allusions may be discerned in other verses. The psalm as a whole was clearly regarded as a source of testimonies to the passion of Christ and His ultimate triumph, and probably from an early date, since it is woven into the texture of the Passion-narrative, and used in writings almost certainly independent of one another. Once again, the sufferings are described as if those of an individual, but with verse 22 interest shifts to the *ecclesia*, and the poem culminates in the proclamation of the universal kingdom of God.

Ps. xxxi has a similar "plot." Verse 13, "They took counsel together against me; they devised to take away my life," has helped to mould Matthew's account of the conspiracy of the Sanhedrin, xxvi. 3-4 (συνήχθησαν, συνεβουλεύσαντο; cf. LXX). Verse 5 is adopted in Lk. xxiii. 46 for the last words of Jesus on the cross. The language of verse 13 seems to be echoed in the gospel accounts of the friends of Jesus gazing from afar at Golgotha, but perhaps xxxviii. 11 and lxxxviii. 8, 18 are even closer to the Gospels (cf. LXX with Lk. xxiii. 49, Mk. xv. 40), and both these psalms belong to the same group, though in lxxxviii the note of ultimate triumph sounds much less clearly.

Ps. xxxiv, on the other hand, while confessing that "many are the afflictions of the righteous," is mainly a song of praise for deliverance achieved, in which the poet treats his own case as typical of the experience of "the righteous" and those who "fear the Lord." The following verses find echo in the New Testament:

xxxiv. 8, "O taste and see . . ." I Pet. ii. 3.

xxxiv. 10 (LXX), πλούσιοι ἐπτώχευσαν καὶ ἐπείνασαν; cf. Lk. i. 53, vi. 24-25.

xxxiv. 12-16, "What man is he that desireth life . . ." I Pet. iii. 10-12.

xxxiv. 20, "He keepeth all his bones; not one of them is broken." In view of the constant use of this group of psalms for *testimonia* of the Passion of Christ, it seems more probable that Jn. xix. 36 draws upon

THE BIBLE OF THE EARLY CHURCH

the present passage than that the reference is to the
paschal victim of Exod. xii. 46. In neither case is
there an exact quotation of the words of the LXX,
but Ps. xxxiv. 20 is slightly nearer to Jn. xix. 36.

xxxiv. 22, λυτροῦν, one of the key words of New Testament thought.

Ps. cxviii similarly consists mainly of praise for the
assured experience of divine deliverance, while recalling
the troubles out of which the Psalmist has been delivered.
Its central theme is the great reversal of fortune (περιπέτεια)
announced in verse 22. It begins with the praises of all
Israel, then gradually contracts, through the House of
Aaron and "those who fear the Lord," to the individual
sufferer—at least in appearance; but when the psalmist
declares, "All nations compassed me about; in the name
of the Lord I will cut them off," it is clear that his attention is in no way confined to an individual case.

The following verses are quoted or echoed in the New
Testament:

cxviii. 10, ἐκύκλωσάν με; cf. Jn. x. 24 (where the "en-
circling" ends in an attempt to arrest Jesus).

cxviii. 16, LXX, δεξιὰ κυρίου ὕψωσέν με, clearly echoed
in Acts ii. 33, τῇ δεξιᾷ τοῦ θεοῦ ὑψωθείς. The
following words, "I shall not die but live," in this context, would readily suggest the resurrection of Christ.

cxviii. 22-23, "the stone which the builders rejected . . ."
quoted in Mk. xii. 10, I Pet. ii. 7, echoed Acts iv. 11;
see pp. 55-56.

cxviii. 25-26, "Save now . . . Blessed be he that cometh
in the name of the Lord," provides the language[1] of
the acclamations of the crowd at Christ's triumphal
entry into Jerusalem, Mk. xi. 9; but is employed also,
Mt. xxiii. 39 = Lk. xiii. 35, in an "eschatological"
context.

[1] With the transliterated Hebrew ὡσαννά in place of the LXX σῶσον δή.

The importance of this psalm as a source of *testimonia* is manifest. The Stone rejected, the Stone of stumbling, the Foundation-stone of Zion, appear to have been associated at a very early stage as symbolic of the coming of Christ and its effects, in various related aspects. The whole psalm was evidently interpreted with reference to the sufferings and rejection of Christ, succeeded by His glorious resurrection and exaltation, all of which is "the Lord's doing, marvellous in our eyes" (23)—to which the psalmist immediately adds, "This is the Day which the Lord has made," which would naturally be understood as indicating that the day of Christ's coming is the prophetic "Day of the Lord." Thus the group of psalms we are studying is linked with the "apocalyptic-eschatological scriptures" of Group I.

I add here three (two) psalms of less importance, which nevertheless played a part in the shaping of Christian thought about Christ's Passion. In each, the original speaks of an individual sufferer.

In Ps. xli, the poet first expresses his confidence in the goodness of God, and then appeals for help in distressing circumstances. In particular, he is the victim of a treacherous friend. Verse 9, which contains this complaint, is quoted in Jn. xiii. 18, under the rubric, ἵνα ἡ γραφὴ πληρωθῇ, with reference to the treachery of Judas. The taunt of the enemy, "Now that he lieth he shall rise up no more," and the sufferer's appeal, "O Lord, raise me up" (ἀνάστησόν με), would in this connection naturally suggest the resurrection of Christ.

Pss. xlii-xliii (properly a single psalm) have for refrain the words, "Why art thou cast down (περίλυπος εἶ), my soul?" (xlii. 5, 11, xliii. 5). This is clearly echoed in Mk. xiv. 34, περίλυπός ἐστιν ἡ ψυχή μου, while Jn. xii. 27, νῦν ἡ ψυχή μου τετάρακται, equally clearly echoes xlii. 6, ἡ ψυχή μου ἐταράχθη. These twin psalms are not psalms of suffering in the same sense as those which we previously examined, but they contain the complaint of one who is shut out from God's presence, but confidently hopes to be restored to it. The evangelists evidently felt that it portrayed one aspect of the Passion of Christ.

With this group I propose to associate Ps. lxxx, in which the "hero" of the "plot" is clearly no individual, but the people of God as a collective whole. It is an appeal to the divine Shepherd—a familiar character in the Gospels—from Israel in distress, exposed to the mockery of their enemies (verse 6, LXX, οἱ ἐχθροὶ ἡμῶν ἐμυκτήρισαν ἡμᾶς cf. ἐξεμυκτήριζον οἱ ἄρχοντες, Lk. xxiii. 35). The poet then describes the fortunes of his people under the allegory of a vine, brought by God out of Egypt and planted. For a time it flourished, but then God broke down the fences of His vineyard, and the wild beasts entered and ravaged it. The poet prays "Look down from heaven and visit this vine" (14). In verse 17 the terms of the prayer change: "Let thy hand be upon the man of thy right hand, upon the son of man who thou madest strong for thyself."

There is here no passage expressly quoted in the New Testament, but the figure of the Vine, which is also the Son of Man and the Man of God's right hand,[1] combines ideas which in the New Testament are so organically united in the person of Christ that it is impossible to suppose the parallel accidental. Indeed, Ps. lxxx. 17, which identifies "God's right-hand Man" (the one who "sits at God's right hand") with the divinely strengthened "Son of Man," might well be regarded as providing direct scriptural

[1] It might be held that the Man is the leader of God's people who are symbolized by the vine, but if so, he is so entirely representative of the people that the two figures coalesce.

justification for the fusion of the two figures in Mk. xiv. 62. More clearly here, perhaps, than anywhere else except in the treatment of Dan. vii, can we see the process by which the corporate and the individual elements are united in early Christian thought about Christ. The Vine with its branches (κλήματα, as in Jn. xv. 2, 5), is the people of God; it is also the Church, and its branches, the disciples of Christ; yet He is Himself the true Vine, in whom alone they become branches or members of the Israel of God. And similarly, Christ is Himself the Son of Man, the Man at God's right hand, and yet the Son of Man is also the true Israel of God. All this seems to be implied in the Christian use of this psalm. It is true that the developed doctrine of the Son of Man who is also the true Vine is found only in the Fourth Gospel.[1] But the title "Son of Man," with its twofold—individual and corporate—connotation, is entirely at home in the Synoptic Gospels, and in Mark and Matthew the cup which contains Christ's "blood of the covenant" contains equally τὸ γένημα τῆς ἀμπέλου (Mk. xiv. 24-25). The identification of the suffering Son of Man with the Vine is not far beneath the surface.

If we now survey this group of scriptures as a whole, we observe that a single "plot" runs all through. The "hero" suffers shame, ignominy, torment, disaster, and then by sheer grace of God is delivered, raised up, glorified. So far, it is the same plot as that which is otherwise presented in scriptures of the first and second groups. But there is this difference to be observed. In Group II, in the main, the suffering and disaster are the judgment of God upon His sinful people, and their restoration is an act of pardon. In Group III, as partly in Group I, the suffering

[1] See *The Interpretation of the Fourth Gospel*, (C. U. P.) pp. 410–412, cf. pp. 246–248.

is, in the main, that of an innocent victim, persecuted by the enemies of God. In some measure, however, the two views of suffering are harmonized in the picture of the Suffering Servant in Is. lii. 13 – liii. 12. The sufferings of the Servant are indeed judgment upon sin, but the sin of others, which he bears vicariously. It is thus possible to recognize Christ as the "hero" of the drama of disaster and triumph in all three groups alike. He is to be identified with the sinful Israel of Hosea, Is. vi-ix and Jer. xxxi in the sense in which the innocent Servant of Is. liii is identified with those whose iniquities he bears, and in His triumph over death and disaster is enacted the promised renovation of the Israel of God, whose sins had brought disaster.

It is this far-reaching identification of Christ, as Son of Man, as Servant, as the righteous Sufferer, with the people of God in all its vicissitudes that justifies the apparent employment by the early Church of Hos. vi. 1-3 as a prophecy of the resurrection of Christ; for the resurrection of Christ *is* the resurrection of Israel of which the prophet spoke. It would also justify Matthew's application of Hos. xi. 1 to Christ. There is nothing here to tell us whether or not we are to accept an exile of Jesus in Egypt as historical fact. If He did indeed suffer such exile, it was not unreasonable for the evangelist to regard it as one more instance of that "recapitulation" of the experience of the people of God in the experience of Christ which is recognized elsewhere. If not, it would be quite understandable that the words of Hosea's prophecy should first have been held to be fulfilled in the deliverance of God's people from bondage, "in Christ" (for the place where the Lord was crucified is "spiritually called Egypt," Rev. xi. 8), and subsequently transferred to Christ himself.

IV. *Unclassified Scriptures*

It remains to bring together, for the sake of completeness, a few passages which do not properly come under any of the above headings.

1. Ps. viii. Of the use of verses 4-6 as a *testimonium* enough has been said (see pp. 32-34). Here we note that verse 2, "Out of the mouths of babes and sucklings hast thou constituted praise" (exactly as in the LXX), is cited in Mt. xxi. 16, with the introduction, οὐδέποτε ἀνέγνωτε; If we suppose the evangelist to have been acquainted with an already established tradition which applied this psalm to the messianic dignity of Jesus, his citation acquires much more force. The acclamations of "Hosanna" (recalling Ps. cxviii. 25), addressed to the King riding into Zion (xxi. 4-5, Zech. ix. 9), who is also the Hero of the grand περιπέτεια of Psalm cxviii (Mt. xxi. 9, 42), are in this case to be understood also as homage to the Son of Man crowned with glory and honour of Ps. viii (for so the evangelist will probably have connected verses 2 and verses 4-6).

2. Ps. cx. The immense importance of verse 1 of this psalm as a *testimonium* has already been discussed (see pp. 34-35). We now note that verse 4 also is employed as a *testimonium* in Heb. v. 6, vi. 20, vii. 17, 21. It is clear from the elaborate argument of which the citation is the basis and centre that the author to the Hebrews is conscious here of being an innovator. Yet his argument rests upon secure grounds if he could count upon the general acceptance of the hundred-and-tenth psalm as being, in its entirety, a testimony to Christ.

3. Some "messianic" scriptures.

Ps. ii. For the use of verse 7 ("Thou art my Son") as a

testimonium see pp. 31-32. Verses 1-2 are quoted (exactly as in the LXX) in Acts iv. 25-26, as that which God "spoke through the holy Spirit by the mouth of David" (if that is what the almost unintelligible Greek was intended to mean), and the quotation is provided with a commentary, pointing out that the "gathering" of kings and rulers against the "anointed" was fulfilled in the plotting of Herod and Pontius Pilate, supported (according to the first verse of the psalm) by the "nations" and the "peoples" of Israel (the plural λαοῖς, unnatural in this connection, being dictated solely by the wording of the psalm), against Jesus, the "anointed" Servant, anointed, we are to understand, with Holy Spirit; cf. Acts. x. 38, after Is. xlii. 1-2, lxi. 1-2, see pp. 52-53).

The continuation of the divine address to the "Son," in verse 9, is taken up in Rev. xii. 5, xix. 15 into the description of the victorious Messiah, while in Rev. ii. 27 the same verse is used as a promise of victory to the faithful servant of Christ—a significant example of the transference of attributes between Christ and the Church, which we note in many places.

It appears then that the whole psalm was regarded as a description of messiahship, fulfilled in the mission and destiny of Jesus. Of all the scriptures we have seen reason for including in the primary body of testimonies this is the only one except Is. ix. 1-7 which is in the proper sense "messianic": the only one, except Is. lxi. 1-2, which speaks of "anointing" at all.

As we have seen, Ps. ii. 7 is cited in Heb. i. 5. It is there associated with II Sam. vii. 14, "I will be to him a father and he shall be to me a son," a passage which, curiously enough, occurs also in a *catena* of scriptural quotations in II Cor. vi. 18 in the form, "I will be to you a father, and you shall be to me sons and daughters"—a remarkable example, again, of the transference of attributes between Christ and the Church.

Neither of these passages betrays any interest in the fact that this promise is originally addressed, in II Sam. vii. 13-14, to the "seed of David," and indeed the idea of the Messiah as son of David is not conspicuous in the primary body of *testimonia*. It is present in Is. ix. 1-7, although the verse which actually mentions the throne of David is not quoted. Acts ii. 30 cites Ps. cxxxii. 11 (in a version slightly differing from the LXX), which speaks of the oath sworn to David that his posterity should sit upon his throne, and employs it (ii. 25-28) to establish the application of Ps. xvi. 8-11 (". . . thou wilt not leave my soul in Hades . . .") to Jesus rather than to David himself, who, as the presumed author of Ps. xvi, might be supposed to be in view. In Acts xiii. 33-37, Ps. ii. 7, Ps. xvi. 10, and Is. lv. 3, δώσω ὑμῖν τὰ ὅσια Δαυεὶδ τὰ πιστά, are associated, as together establishing the messiahship of the risen Jesus. To these passages we should add the citation in Acts xv. 16-17 of Amos ix. 11-12 (with some introductory words from Jer. xii. 15), "I will rebuild the fallen tent of David . . ." said to be fulfilled in the gathering of Gentiles into the Church.

It appears, then, that we have here a combination of selected extracts from passages of scripture which were not otherwise exploited. It is noteworthy that in so far as they explicitly refer to the Messiah Son of David they are confined to the Acts. That the Davidic descent of Jesus was affirmed in the *kerygma* we have good reason to believe: it not only appears in the kerygmatic passages of Acts, but also in the brief confession of faith in Rom. i. 3-4, although Paul elsewhere betrays no interest in it. But so far as our evidence goes, it does not appear that it played any great part in the shaping of Christian theology.

4. There remain only two of our fifteen primary *testimonia* which we have not yet examined in their scriptural context: the promise to Abraham, Gen. xii. 3, xxii. 18 (see pp. 43-44) and the prediction of the "prophet like Moses" in Deut. xviii. 15, 19 (see pp. 53-57). The result of such examination is negative. In each case the passage cited is isolated, and the context in which it occurs is not otherwise employed to elucidate the ideas of the *kerygma*. The prediction of the "prophet like Moses" had little significance for the development of New Testament theology. The story of Abraham in a general way is in the background of many passages of the New Testament, but apart from the promise of the blessing of the Gentiles it does not appear that particular passages from it were employed to elucidate the *kerygma*.[1]

At this point it will be convenient to have before us a conspectus of the passages we have been considering.

Primary sources of testimonies	*Subordinate and supplementary sources*
I. Joel ii-iii; Zech. ix-xiv; Dan. vii.	Mal. iii. 1-6; Dan. xii.
II. Hosea, Is. vi. 1 — ix. 7, xi. 1-10, xxviii. 16, xl. 1-11; Jer. xxxi. 10-34.	Is. xxix. 9-14; Jer. vii. 1-15; Hab. i-ii.

[1] The citation of Gen. xv. 6 in Jas. ii. 23. Rom. iv. 3, 9, 22, is not in point. This belongs to a discussion upon the nature and efficacy of "faith," which we know to have gone on in Judaism (from Philo and IV Ezra, e.g.), before it was taken up on new ground in the Church. The discussion does not bear directly upon the understanding of the *kerygma*.

Primary sources of testimonies	*Subordinate and supplementary sources*
III. Is. xlii. 1 — xliv. 5, xlix. 1-13, l. 4-11, lii. 13 — liii. 12, lxi. Ps. lxix, xxii, xxxi, xxxviii, lxxxviii, xxxiv, cxviii, xli, xlii-xliii, lxxx.	Is. lviii. 6-10.
IV. Ps. viii, cx, ii. Gen. xii. 3, xxii. 18. Deut. xviii. 15, 19.	Ps. cxxxii, xvi; II Sam. vii. 13-14; Is. lv. 3; Amos, ix. 11-12.

It is not pretended that this is an exhaustive list of scriptures in which the early Church found testimonies to the facts declared in the *kerygma*, but I believe that these passages have qualified, after a somewhat searching examination, for a position in any such list. The writings of the New Testament which have been adduced in evidence are of various dates, some early, some later: that all of them directly attest a primitive use of these scriptures could not be maintained. It is the coincidence of evidence from different quarters that carries weight. In any case, the selection and presentation of *testimonia* was not a static achievement, but a process, and one which continued well through the New Testament period and beyond. But in most of the cases we have examined there seemed to be good reason to infer that the first step, at least, had been taken by the Church at a very early stage indeed, often demonstrably earlier than the epistles of Paul. At the earliest period of Church history to which we can gain access, we find in being the rudiments of an original, coherent and flexible method of biblical exegesis which was already beginning to yield results.

If we ask further questions about the actual beginnings of the process, we are on much more uncertain ground, but some degree of controlled conjecture may be allowed. It must be conceded that we have before us a considerable intellectual feat. The various scriptures are acutely interpreted along lines already discernible within the Old Testament canon itself or in pre-Christian Judaism—in many cases, I believe, lines which start from their first, historical, intention—and these lines are carried forward to fresh results. Very diverse scriptures are brought together so that they interpret one another in hitherto unsuspected ways. To have brought together, for example, the Son of Man who is the people of the saints of the Most High, the Man of God's right hand, who is also the vine of Israel, the Son of Man who after humiliation is crowned with glory and honour, and the victorious priest-king at the right hand of God, is an achievement of interpretative imagination which results in the creation of an entirely new figure. It involves an original, and far-reaching, resolution of the tension between the individual and the collective aspects of several of these figures, which in turn makes it possible to bring into a single focus the "plot" of the Servant poems of II Isaiah, of the psalms of the righteous sufferer, and of the prophecies of the fall and recovery (death and resurrection) of the people of God, and finally offers a fresh understanding of the mysterious imagery of apocalyptic eschatology.

This is a piece of genuinely creative thinking. Who was responsible for it? The early Church, we are accustomed to say, and perhaps we can safely say no more. But creative thinking is rarely done by committees, useful as they may be for systematizing the fresh ideas of individual thinkers, and for stimulating them to further thought.

H

It is individual minds that originate. Whose was the originating mind here?

Among Christian thinkers of the first age known to us there are three of genuinely creative power: Paul, the author to the Hebrews, and the Fourth Evangelist. We are precluded from proposing any one of them for the honour of having originated the process, since even Paul, greatly as he contributed to its development, demonstrably did not originate it. What forgotten geniuses may lurk in the shadows of those first twenty years of Church history about which we are so scantily informed, it is impossible for us to say. But the New Testament itself avers that it was Jesus Christ Himself who first directed the minds of His followers to certain parts of the scriptures as those in which they might find illumination upon the meaning of His mission and destiny. That He formally set before them a comprehensive scheme of biblical interpretation, after the manner of Lk. xxiv. 25-27, 44-45, we may well hesitate to believe; but I can see no reasonable ground for rejecting the statements of the Gospels that (for example) He pointed to Psalm cx as a better guide to the truth about His mission and destiny than the popular beliefs about the Son of David, or that He made that connection of the "Lord" at God's right hand with the Son of Man in Daniel which proved so momentous for Christian thought; or that He associated with the Son of Man language which had been used of the Servant of the Lord, and employed it to hint at the meaning, and the issue, of His own approaching death. To account for the beginning of this most original and fruitful process of re-thinking the Old Testament we found need to postulate a creative mind. The Gospels offer us one. Are we compelled to reject the offer?

IV

FUNDAMENTALS OF CHRISTIAN
THEOLOGY

WE have now in some measure clarified the meaning of the affirmation that the evangelical facts took place "according to the scriptures." We have been able to answer with some degree of precision the question, "What scriptures?" We have examined the principles of selection and exegesis employed. In what now follows I shall try to show that the fundamental and regulative ideas of Christian theology as it meets us in the New Testament arise directly out of the understanding of these scriptures in relation to the evangelical facts.

I. *The Church*

In the application of *testimonia* from the Old Testament, it is a fundamental postulate that the Church is the true, and ultimate, people of God, the heir of the divinely-guided history of Israel, which emerged out of the crisis in which God visited his people in judgment and redemption. Out of this conviction arose the whole Christian doctrine of the Church. It explains the extraordinary confidence and audacity with which a small group of obscure individuals embraced such an immense task as that which the early Christian community undertook, and to so large an extent carried through. In imaginative reconstructions of the first age of the Church we have often been presented with the picture of a group of puzzled Galileans huddled together for mutual support and encouragement, and coming to form one of the many groups or sects within the Jewish community, without any idea that they were anything more, until with the gradual emergence of other similar groups a kind of *esprit de corps* arose, and persecution drove them into closer association, and so by degrees they achieved a doctrine of the one Church, as it meets us, for example, in the Epistle to the Ephesians.

A study of the primitive *testimonia* shows that this picture is out of focus. From as early a stage as we can hope to reach (presupposed already by Paul) the primitive Christians were aware that they belonged to the new "Israel of God," which had emerged, as the prophets had always said it would, out of judgment and disaster. It was the true *ecclesia*, or people of God, by definition single and unique, one in all the earth. The universality of the ultimate people of God is an integral feature of the final *dénouement* in various prophetic passages, notably in those of Joel, Zechariah, and II Isaiah. If the precise position of Gentile believers in the Church was at first somewhat ambiguous, this ambiguity is already present in the prophecies. Paul forced the Church to draw the logical conclusions from its doctrine of the new "eschatological" Israel, but it is highly improbable that he invented that doctrine. Nor is it likely, although his wider outlook gave him an acuter sense of the paradox involved in attaching the attributes of the ultimate people of God to a community of "the weak, the ignoble, the despised— sheer non-entities" (cf. I Cor. i. 27-28), that he was the first to be aware of the paradox. For the first Christians the emergence of the Church as the new Israel was sheer miracle from the hand of God ("It is the Lord's doing, and it is marvellous in our eyes," Ps. cxviii. 23; Mk. xii. 11, etc.). In plain fact, its foundation-members were disgraced and discredited men until the risen Christ raised them up. We ought never to forget this: it is pertinent to all our discussions about the nature of the Church.

If then the whole episode of the beginnings of Christianity is to be understood, as the first Christians understood it, in the light of prophecy, what happened was that the existing Jewish community ceased to represent the true Israel of God, as the embodiment of His purposes for mankind, and its place was taken by the Christian *ecclesia*. The new community did not take this historical position because its members were wiser, more virtuous, or more capable than their Jewish contemporaries, but because they had been the objects of an act of God. The crucial moment in the whole episode, and its operative centre, was the passion, death, and resurrection of Jesus Christ. It is in Him that what is essential in the prophecies of the true Israel (the Servant of the Lord, the Son of Man) found fulfilment. In Him the whole Israel of God was incorporate. Its destiny was wrought out in His experience. In Him the people of God was judged, died and rose to newness of life. Thus whatever may be predicated of the Church is predicated of it only as its members are incorporate in Christ as their "inclusive representative." Hence the Pauline "in Christ" is strictly congruous with primitive Christian conceptions. To be "crucified with Christ," to be "risen with Him": these ideas are no inventions of Paul's fertile genius, and certainly no mere rhetorical flourishes. That is what the Church is, by definition. Each of its members is such by virtue of this *koinonia* with Christ. Similarly, the Johannine conception of the vine and the branches comes directly out of primitive Christian thought; and in fact out of Ps. lxxx, which was an important source for testimonies; for it speaks of a "Son of Man" who may also be represented as the vine which God himself brought out of Egypt and planted. There is some likelihood that at a date earlier than the Fourth Gospel the idea had already entered into the liturgy, if the eucharistic prayers in the *Didaché* are indeed early (as they almost certainly are, whatever date we assign to the compilation); and it may have been through the liturgy that it entered into Johannine theology.

II. *The Messianic Titles*

The foundations of Christology have been sought in various directions.

(1) It has been held that "the Jewish doctrine of the Messiah" was simply transferred to Jesus, and that Christology ramified from this source. But in fact there was at the beginning of the first century, so far as our information goes, no such thing as "the Jewish doctrine of the Messiah." The term מְשִׁיחַ, מְשִׁיחָא, χριστός, was a vague though extremely honorific title, applied (e.g.) to historical princes of the house of David, to the reigning High Priest, and to various ideal figures, past, or yet to come. It was not until after the fall of the Temple, perhaps not until the second century, that there was any clearly formulated, and generally accepted, messianic dogma. The Church was the first to put forward a definite and coherent doctrine of the Messiah, and it was unlike the messianic doctrine which ultimately emerged in Judaism.

(2) Others, recognizing that Jewish messianic ideas afford an insufficient basis for the Church's Christology in its early forms, have looked for its origins in Hellenistic

conceptions, especially those associated with mystery-cults, and those characteristic of the "Hellenistic mysticism" of such writings as the *Hermetica* (presupposed also in the writings of Philo the Jew). That such conceptions had an influence on the development of Christian theology is on all counts probable. But the fundamentals of New Testament Christology can be traced back to a stage when Hellenistic influence was at a minimum.

(3) At a time well within the memory of many of us, about the turn of the century, there was a movement to establish Christology afresh upon the basis of "the messianic self-consciousness of Jesus." It was thought that by scrutinizing the Gospels for evidence of this "self-consciousness" we might by-pass the supposedly alien influences, Jewish and Hellenistic, that diverted Christian belief from its true course, and draw a purer doctrine direct from the fountain-head. The outcome of the attempt was not encouraging; and indeed it rested upon a misapprehension of the nature of our sources for the life of Jesus. How much the beliefs of our earliest witnesses about their Master owed to any partial disclosures of His own inner life that may have been allowed them, it is impossible to say. What they have given us is a report of what He overtly did and said, vitalized by the ubiquitous effects of the faith which He had awakened in them, and which alone gave them understanding of His words and deeds.

The foundations of the Church's Christology can more hopefully be sought in the application of prophecy in the earliest period accessible to us, because this represents the way in which the first witnesses found the clue to the meaning of events, and of words and deeds of their Master, which admittedly had eluded their understanding in His lifetime.

If we scrutinize the scriptures which formed the main sources of *testimonia*, a remarkably small proportion of them are found to be explicitly "messianic," either in the sense that they contain the title "Messiah" ("the Lord's Anointed"), or that they can be shown to have received a messianic interpretation in pre-Christian Judaism. The outstanding titles which are transferred from prophecy to the *kerygma* concerning Jesus are "Son of Man" and "Servant." It is noteworthy that neither of these titles came to be of first-rate importance in the developed theology of the Church. Both belong characteristically to the primitive stage.

The title "Son of Man" is often said to be the title of the "apocalyptic Messiah" of pre-Christian Judaism. The sole evidence for this figure is in the so-called "Similitudes of Enoch," i.e. chapters xxxvii-lxx of the Ethiopic Book of Enoch. These chapters have not so far been found in any of the now fairly extensive Greek fragments of the Book of Enoch. There are three different Ethiopic expressions which are supposed to be equivalent to the single Greek expression which we translate "Son of Man"; whether they can all be accepted as such is not fully clear. Nor is their precise meaning certain. Some take them to be other names for the personage otherwise called "the Elect One"; others as denominating a personification of "the elect" (plural). Lacking a Greek text, we cannot be certain how much of this part of the Ethiopic Enoch genuinely represents an earlier original. Where we are able to test the Ethiopic text in other parts of the work, it does not suggest great confidence. Until we know more about this, it cannot be accepted as certain that the Similitudes are pre-Christian at all. However this may be, the Similitudes are in any case an isolated and probably eccentric authority for the association of the title "Son of Man" with an "apocalyptic Messiah," and cannot be used with any confidence to elucidate the New Testament.

There are three passages in Scripture containing the term "Son of Man," and three only,[1] which can be *proved* to have been employed for testimonies: Ps. viii, Ps. lxxx and Dan. vii. Of these, Dan. vii and Ps. lxxx are about the fortunes of Israel, first oppressed, humiliated and all but destroyed by the enemies of God, and then delivered and raised to great glory by his power and mercy. In Ps. viii the "son of man" (in parallelism with "man") is simply man as such, man in his weakness and insignificance, yet "visited" by God, and by his merciful ordinance "crowned with glory and honour." There is a clear analogy with the "Son of Man" of Ps. lxxx and Dan. vii,[2] which speak of Israel, under the similitude of a human figure, humiliated into insignificance until visited by God and raised to glory.

In these three passages, therefore, the "Son of Man" is a figure representative of a community, which may be Israel, as the people of God, or mankind, as "visited" by God. If we take seriously the universality of the "eschatological" people of God, then the idea of humanity as redeemed by God's grace may be recognized in both.

[1] The frequently recurrent "Son of Man" in Ezekiel may no doubt have been in the minds of early Christians, but proof that it was so is lacking in the New Testament. Ezekiel does not appear to have been a primary source of testimonies.

[2] It is not always observed that the implication of the vision of the beasts and the figure "like a son of man" is that there has been a period in which the beasts (the pagan empires) were rampant, and the son of man (the people of the saints of the Most High) was oppressed; nor must this vision be separated from that in ch. ii. Now the tables are turned. The beasts vanish and the Son of Man is supreme; as in Ps. viii man, by God's merciful ordinance, is given sovereignty over the animal creation. To say, as it is often said, that the Old Testament knows nothing of a suffering Son of Man is inaccurate.

The New Testament use of the title "Son of Man" for Christ results from the individuation of this corporate conception. "In Christ," mankind is delivered and exalted by the visitation of God, and becomes a people of the saints of the Most High.

The term "Servant (of the Lord)" is used of Christ in primitive kerygmatic passages (Acts iii. 13, 26, iv. 27, 30),[1] and it long survived in liturgical usage. In the relevant passages of II Isaiah its meaning oscillates between the individual and the corporate. The Servant is either a pure personification of Israel (or of the faithful remnant of Israel), like the Son of Man of Daniel and probably of Ps. lxxx, or else he is an individual whose experience in humiliation and in glory is vicarious; or in other words, who fulfils representatively the destiny of Israel in suffering and in resurrection to newness of life. In the New Testament this ambiguity is overcome. The role of the Servant in its completeness is personally enacted by Christ crucified and risen, but His experience is no less corporate. In Him the people of God passes through disaster to glory. The possibility of a real (and not either abstract or fictitious) "representation" of the many by the one is given in the idea of a voluntary act of self-sacrifice such as is adumbrated in Is. liii and made actual in the self-sacrifice of Jesus. As Servant, he deliberately

---

[1] It has been argued that the use of the term παῖς in such passages is secondary, since it comes out of the LXX, and consequently implies a Hellenistic Christianity. Upon this I would remark (1) that to get back to a stage at which there were *no* Greek-speaking Christians is a hopeless enterprise, if there is any truth in Acts vi. 1; (2) the identification of Jesus with the Servant does not depend on the occurrence of the term παῖς in particular passages (the LXX also uses δοῦλος for עֶבֶד—and so does Paul in Phil. ii. 7). It is presupposed in the application of almost every verse of Is. lii. 13-liii. 12, as well as of several verses from other "Servant" passages, to Christ, in places covering almost all New Testament writings.

associates himself with sinful humanity and offers his life as λύτρον ἀντὶ πολλῶν (Mk. x. 45).

It appears, then, that it is a central feature of the Christian idea of Messiahship that the Messiah is "inclusive representative" of the people of God, which in His person passes through the experience of death and resurrection by which it secures existence as an actual community of living men. Christology, it is not too much to say, is rooted in the understanding of the passion, death and resurrection of Jesus in the light of a combination of the ideas of Son of Man and Servant.[1] This combination of ideas can be traced to the most primitive period accessible to us.

This conception of the Messiah as the "inclusive representative" of the people of God is combined with another view which sets him over against God's people as its Lord or anointed King. Here the idea of messianic kingship, as found notably in Ps. ii and Zech. ix. 9, forms the basis for Christology. The title "king" itself is seldom directly applied to Christ, except in the Passion-narrative, where it is rendered inevitable by hard historical fact. Yet there are passages which betray the familiarity of the idea among early Christians. (Note especially Mt. xxv. 31-34, where the Son of Man is also the King; Rev. xix. 16; and the curious passage Acts xvii. 7, which suggests a reason why we do not find the title more frequently in our authorities; to these we must add passages which speak of the "kingdom" of Christ, or of the Son of Man: Mt. xiii. 41, I Cor. xv. 24.) At the crucial point, the kingship of Christ is emphatically dissociated from the

[1] As we have seen, it is not quite accurate to say that the Old Testament knows nothing of a suffering Son of Man; but it is only when he is identified with the Servant that the sufferings of the Son of Man can be considered redemptive.

messianic kingship as understood in popular Judaism of the time. In Mk. xii. 35-37 the Messiah Son of David, that is to say, the expected political sovereign of Israel in the legitimate line, is expressly distinguished from the person addressed in Ps. cx. Historically, no doubt, this psalm was written for a victorious prince. But the first century, no longer at home with the oriental imagery of the psalm, could not understand the expression "Sit thou at my right hand" as applicable to any earthly prince. The throne of God is in the spiritual realm; to sit at His right hand is to share His spiritual authority. Accordingly, the expression "till I make thy enemies the footstool of thy feet" was interpreted as referring to the spiritual powers of evil, overcome by Christ through His cross. In this sense it was early associated with Ps. viii. 5-6 (see I Cor. xv. 25-27, where the two passages are cited in close connection; cf. also Heb. i. 13, ii. 9). So understood, Ps. cx. 1 supplied the standing formula for the exaltation of the risen Christ, which is an inseparable article of the *kerygma* in all its forms and passed thence into the Creed: "He sitteth at the right hand of God."

Now, this passage, Ps. cx. 1, speaks of the Person seated at God's right hand as "Lord." And it was this appellation, rather than "King," which came into use to designate the Messiah when he is set over against the People of God as its sovereign Ruler.[1] It has been widely held that the use of this title is due to the familiar use of the Greek κύριος in pagan cults of the Hellenistic world,[2] and consequently

[1] Occasionally we find *archon* or *archegos* as alternative equivalents for "king," Acts v. 31, Rev. i. 5; somewhat differently, Acts iii. 15, Heb. ii. 10, xii. 2; but *kyrios* seems to have over-shadowed all other such titles from the beginning.

[2] The question of the origin of such Hellenistic usages needs more attention that it sometimes receives. It is not Hellenic, but owes something, apparently, to Egypt and to Semitic sources. It is not certain

that it is not primitive.[1] There can be little doubt that various Hellenistic usages affected the development of the idea of Christ as *Kyrios* in early Christian theology and even in the New Testament itself. But since the title "Lord" is given to Christ in a *testimonium* which is as clearly primitive as anything we have, it seems unnecessary to go farther for the origin of the usage, however it may have been extended and enriched in meaning from other sources.

In primitive Christian messianic doctrine, then, there are these two inseparable moments: the Messiah is identified with the People of God as their "inclusive representative": he is set over against the People of God as sovereign Lord.

We may find here a basis for a large part of the developed Christology of Paul. His doctrine of the heavenly Man, or Second Adam, has behind it the primitive "Son of Man" Christology. The heavenly Man is the "new man" which the believer assumes in becoming a member of the Church, and the "perfect man" into which the entire Church grows up (Col. iii. 10-11; Eph. iv. 13). Hence the Church is the "body" of Christ; in two senses: (1) the Church is the body of Christ in such a sense that it can be said, "As the body is one and has many members, so also is *Christ*" (I Cor. xii. 12), or, "We being many are one body *in Christ*" (Rom. xii. 5), i.e. Christ is in some sort identified with the body; (2) Christ is distinguished from the body as its "Head," the seat of authority over the whole (Eph. i. 22-23, etc.). As such he is Κύριος. This

that the κύριος of the LXX is a pure piece of Hellenization or that it was entirely without influence upon certain Hellenistic circles. See my book *The Bible and the Greeks*, pp. 8-11.

[1] In any case, as I observed with reference to παῖς, the idea that we could get back to a primitive period when there were *no* Greek-speaking persons in the Church is chimerical.

title has in Paul a greatly extended range, but it clearly starts from Ps. cx. 1, which he links inseparably with Ps. viii. 6 in the passage about the heavenly Man in I Cor. xv. 25-27.

In the Epistle to the Hebrews the same fundamental scriptures recur, and in the same combination. In the great Christological affirmation with which the epistle opens, the Lord at God's right hand (i. 13) and the Son of Man crowned with glory and honour because of the suffering of death (ii. 9) are inseparable aspects of a unitary conception, and they are linked with more narrowly messianic *testimonia* from II Sam. vii. 14 and Ps. ii (i. 5). This writer, however, has brought out a feature of Ps. cx. not apparently noticed at an earlier stage: the Lord at God's right hand is also "priest for ever after the order of Melchidezek." Reflection upon this has led him to the idea of the two orders or planes of being, represented by the two priesthoods, that of Aaron and that of Melchidezek, and hence to a highly original doctrine of Christ as the eternal High Priest. This doctrine is worked out on Platonizing lines, but its starting point lies clearly within the primitive body of *testimonia*.

In the Fourth Gospel, again, the idea of the Son of Man is fundamental, and while it has absorbed elements from Hellenistic thought about the heavenly or "essential Man" it is at bottom the concept which results from a combination of Ps. viii, Ps. lxxx, Dan. vii, and Is. liii. The ideas of corporate representation and of glory through suffering, which, as we have seen, are regulative from the first, here receive highly original treatment. In particular, the evangelist brings into full clarity the truth that the Servant is "exalted and greatly glorified" (Is. lii. 13, LXX) *in* his sufferings and death, and that it is through dying that he incorporates men in himself, "that they may all be one." (Jn. xii. 32, xvii. 21).[1]

These brief pointers must suffice to indicate the way in which even the most original and individual developments of Christology in the New Testament remain rooted in the primitive body of testimonies from the Old Testament, considered as declaring "the determinate counsel of God," now fulfilled in the evangelical facts.

III. *The Doctrine of the Death of Christ*

It is often assumed that there was a time when the Church could think of the cross only as a disaster retrieved by the resurrection, and that only subsequent reflection found a positive meaning in it. It is impossible to deny that this may have been so; but if there was such a period, it is a period to which we have no access. At the earliest stage to which the evidence enables us to go back, Jesus is already thought of as the "Servant" of Is. lii. 13 – liii. 12, whose death in utter obedience to God is for the redemption of the "many," and issues in glory and exaltation. This scripture at once suggests two moments in the meaning of the death of Christ. (1) The Servant incorporates in himself the whole people of God; his death therefore is their death; his resurrection their resurrection. His death therefore is vicarious, or more properly representative. (2) As such it is an "offering for sin." It expiates sin by exhausting its consequences. It is to be observed that this representative character of expiatory sacrifice is intrinsic to the whole idea of such sacrifice. Such a sacrifice (in ancient thought) is valid in so far as there is solidarity between victim and worshipper. The second Isaiah, and after him the early Church, do complete justice to this

[1] See my book, *The Interpretation of the Fourth Gospel*, pp. 247-248.

antique idea in the process of sublimating or "etherializing" it.

There is a further point. In Is. xlii. 6, xlix. 8, the Servant is "given for a covenant of the people." Although in lii. 13 – liii. 12 his death is not connected with the establishment of the covenant, the connection is easily made. When the scriptures of the Servant of the Lord were brought together with other prophecies, as with that of Zech. ix, where the King who comes in humility to liberate the prisoners and to speak peace to the nations is associated with the idea of the "blood of the covenant," then it was almost inevitable that the death of the Servant should be thought of as a covenant-sacrifice. Through his death a covenant was established by which a "people of the saints of the Most High" came into being—a people incorporate in the Servant as Son of Man, and drawing its character therefrom.

The fact that another of the regulative *testimonia*— Jeremiah's prophecy of the New Covenant—gave the forgiveness of sins as an essential feature of that covenant, made it again an easy step to connect the Servant's "offering for sin" with the covenant-sacrifice.[1] This connection of ideas, in fact, provides the basis for the whole New Testament doctrine of the atoning death of Christ, so variously developed in Paul, the Epistle to the Hebrews, and the Gospel and Epistles of John. This doctrine, though it ramified in all directions, is an integral part of the earliest Christian theological thinking to which we have access, and no afterthought.[2]

[1] We have seen that the combination early entered into liturgical expression: see Mt. xxvi. 28, as compared with other forms of the Words of Institution.

[2] It is noteworthy that the nearer we approach to the earliest attested starting point, the less support is to be found for a purely "Abelardian" interpretation of the Atonement.

Both these ideas are metaphors drawn from ancient ritual, and as such the most expressive metaphors the mind of antiquity could command. But it is of the greatest importance that both these metaphors entered into Christian theology through a medium which gives them the reality of personal action. The picture of the death of the Servant in Is. lii. 13 – liii. 12 has traits drawn from the ritual of expiatory sacrifice, but it emerges as a picture of human and personal *self*-sacrifice. It is because he is God's loyal Servant that he voluntarily bears the sin of the many, pours out his soul unto death, and makes intercession for the transgressors; and that God accepts his self-sacrifice as an "offering for sin" through which the many are redeemed. This crucial feature, of voluntary self-sacrifice, has passed fully into the New Testament employment of this scripture for the explication of the death of Christ. Through all elaboration of sacrificial metaphors, all our New Testament theologians—Paul, the author to the Hebrews, and John alike—constantly emphasize the *obedience* of Christ (obedience, says Paul, like that of a δοῦλος) as the operative factor in His sacrifice.

I

V

CONCLUSIONS

THE argument of the three foregoing chapters has led to results which may be summarized as follows:

1. The quotation of passages from the Old Testament (whether or not under a formula of quotation) is not to be accounted for by the postulate of a primitive anthology of isolated proof-texts. The composition of "testimony-books" was the result, not the presupposition, of the work of early Christian biblical scholars. The evidence suggests that at a very early date a certain *method* of biblical study was established and became part of the equipment of Christian evangelists and teachers. This method was largely employed orally, and found literary expression only sporadically and incompletely, but it is presupposed in our earliest sources.

2. The method included, first, the *selection* of certain large sections of the Old Testament scriptures, especially from Isaiah, Jeremiah and certain minor prophets, and from the Psalms. These sections were understood as *wholes*, and particular verses or sentences were quoted from them rather as pointers to the whole context than as constituting testimonies in and for themselves. At the same time, detached sentences from other parts of the Old Testament could be adduced to illustrate or elucidate the meaning of the main section under consideration. But in the fundamental passages it is the *total context* that is in view, and is the basis of the argument.

3. The relevant scriptures were understood and interpreted upon intelligible and consistent principles, as

setting forth "the determinate counsel of God" which was
fulfilled in the gospel facts, and consequently as fixing
the meaning of those facts.

4. This whole body of material—the passages of Old
Testament scripture with their application to the gospel
facts—is common to all the main portions of the New
Testament, and in particular it provided the starting
point for the theological constructions of Paul, the author
to the Hebrews, and the Fourth Evangelist. It is the
substructure of all Christian theology and contains already
its chief regulative ideas.

The question must now be raised, whether the principles
and methods followed by the early oral tradition of Old
Testament interpretation lying behind the New Testament
have continuing validity as a means to the theological
understanding of the gospel facts. Our study of the treatment of *testimonia* will at any rate have shown that the
New Testament writers do not, in the main, treat the
prophecies of the Old Testament as a kind of pious fortune-
telling, and seek to impress their readers with the exact-
ness of correspondence between forecast and event. This
kind of argument was freely used by Christian apologists
at a somewhat later period, but it is less convincing to us
than it presumably was to its original public. It is not
entirely absent from the New Testament. It seems clear,
for example, that the Matthaean version of the story of
the Triumphal Entry of Christ into Jerusalem has introduced a second donkey, where Mark has only one, in order
to exhibit an exact correspondence with the actual wording of Zech. ix. 9.[1] But instances of this kind are rare,

[1] This modification must apparently have been the work of someone
who did not understand the nature of Hebrew parallelism.

and have been given an altogether disproportionate emphasis in discussions of the subject. Certainly in the body of *testimonia* which we are entitled to regard as primitive this particular motive, if not absent, is always subordinate. To carry into our study of the New Testament even a half-unconscious expectation of finding everywhere this dubious factor at work is to prepare for inevitable misunderstanding.

The assumption which the New Testament writers do make is a different one. They interpret and apply the prophecies of the Old Testament upon the basis of a certain understanding of history, which is substantially that of the prophets themselves. Though not stated explicitly in the New Testament it is everywhere pre-supposed. History, upon this view, or at any rate the history of the people of God, is built upon a certain pattern corresponding to God's design for man His creature. It is a pattern, not in the sense of a pre-ordained sequence of inevitable events, but in the sense of a kind of master-plan imposed upon the order of human life in this world by the Creator Himself, a plan which man is not at liberty to alter, but within which his freedom works. It is this pattern, disclosed "in divers parts and divers manners" in the past history of Israel, that the New Testament writers conceive to have been brought into full light in the events of the gospel story, which they interpret accordingly.

This is a view of history which merits consideration in its own right. It coheres with the entire Hebrew-Christian *Weltanschauung:* its conception of the nature of man, of the relations between man and the universe, and of the relation of both to their Creator. Its specific character emerges when we compare and contrast it with some rival views, for example the theory of recurrent historical cycles,

dominant in antiquity and formulated in masterly fashion
by Plato, or the nineteenth-century theory of progressive
development on the lines of biological evolution. For the
prophetic view no such simple diagram as a circle or an
ascending curve or straight line is appropriate, since it
deals in personal relations not susceptible to diagram-
matic formulation. The prophets saw history as the field
upon which the living God perpetually confronts man with
a challenge. To this challenge he must respond; his choice
is free, but free within limits; and by his response he
helps to shape the course of events to ends beyond his
surmising.

Thus the prophets deny that history moves under its
own steam, that man has in himself power to direct it,
and in general that the movement of history can be
understood entirely within, and out of, itself. There is a
mysterious factor, praeter-human and praeter-natural,
which is real and powerful, and without the recognition of
this factor history remains unintelligible. This supra-
historical factor in history is the living God Himself. His
impact upon human society reveals itself negatively as
judgment upon human action, positively as power of
renewal, or redemption. This twofold rhythm of the pattern of history finds characteristic expression in terms
of death and resurrection. This, and neither cyclic recurrence nor linear development, is the real nature of historical action.

Such was the meaning which the prophets distilled out
of the tragic course of events in which they were partakers.
They bore witness that it would emerge fully only
in an event in which absolute judgment and absolute
redemption should become actual among men. Taking
up this view of history the earliest thinkers of Christianity
declared that in the ministry, death and resurrection of

Jesus Christ this act of absolute judgment and absolute redemption had taken place. This complex event therefore becomes the centre from which the whole history of the people of God, both backwards and forwards in time, is to be understood, and ultimately the history of all mankind.

This is the assumption which underlies the application of Old Testament prophecy to the gospel facts. Stated in those terms it is bald and abstract; but if we follow the guidance of the New Testament writers, and study those parts of the Old Testament to which they refer us, sympathetically, with an open mind, having always before us in imagination the story of the Gospels, we shall find that they penetrate in a variety of ways, and in differing detail, into the real, permanent moral situation of men in history, and so to our own situation.

In general, then, the writers of the New Testament, in making use of passages from the Old Testament, remain true to the main intention of their writers. Yet the actual meaning discovered in a given passage will seldom, in the nature of things, coincide precisely with that which it had in its original context. The transposition into a fresh situation involves a certain shift, nearly always an expansion, of the original scope of the passage. There are prophecies interpreted "messianically" in the New Testament where it is a matter of dispute whether or not the Old Testament writer had any intention to foretell the coming of a person bearing the character and functions which came to be designated by the term "Messiah," or indeed had in mind any personage of the future at all. Among passages important from the first as a source of testimonies, Ps. ii is only one out of many scriptures which have been, and still are, variously understood by scholars as referring to an historical monarch or to an ideal figure

of the future.[1] Ps. cx, again, is generally understood
to have been originally a song for the enthronement of
some victorious Israelite or Jewish ruler whose period has
not yet been determined. But both these psalms are
confidently treated by our authors as prophecies of Christ.
Still clearer is it that Ps. viii has been subject to reinterpretation. In its original intention it is a poem upon
the startling contrast between man's position in the
universe as lord of creation and his insignificance in the
sight of God, the contradiction being resolved by the
recognition that man is whatever he may be, solely as the
object of God's care, and because God willed it so: his
littleness and his greatness alike testify to the glory of
God—a fundamental idea which in one form or another
runs all through the Bible. But as applied in the New
Testament this psalm becomes the vehicle of a singularly
profound conception of what messiahship means, a conception, we must suppose, strange to the ancient Hebrew
poet.

To recognize all this is not to deny validity to the New
Testament interpretation of the Old Testament. It would
not be true of any literature which deserves to be called
great, that its meaning is restricted to that which was
explicitly in the mind of the author when he wrote. On
the contrary, it is a part of what constitutes the quality of
greatness in literature that it perpetuates itself by unfold-
ing ever new richness of unsuspected meaning as time
goes on. The ultimate significance of prophecy is not only
what it meant for its author, but what it came to mean
for those who stood within the tradition which he founded

[1] According to the Scandinavian school, this and other "messianic"
scriptures have behind them the ritual myth of the Divine King.
Upon this view the alternative—"historical" or "eschatological"?—
is no longer exclusive.

or promoted, and who lived under the impact of the truth he declared. It is a thoroughly unhistorical proceeding to attempt to read the biblical documents as if they were (let us say) newly discovered Ugaritic texts, coming to us out of a forgotten age, across an unbridged chasm of time. They have had a continuous life within the community to which they belong, and belonged from the first, in its changing forms, Israelite, Jewish and Christian. The Old Testament Scriptures formed part of the daily environment of the writers of the New Testament, as the writings of both testaments form part of our own daily environment in the Christian Church. The meaning of the writings cannot remain static while the life to which they belong changes with the centuries.

In saying this, I do not mean to suggest that the plain, original meaning of the documents, as it may be recovered by the most searching historical criticism, is unimportant, or that any and every reinterpretation, the product of profound insight, of mistaken ingenuity, or of mere fancy, is equally legitimate or equally valid, even if the interpreter be a canonical writer himself. I am only concerned to disarm the prejudice which has long haunted critical studies (understandable enough as a reaction from earlier exaggerations)—the prejudice that the treatment of the Old Testament in the New is in principle of no more than antiquarian interest, and incapable of making any serious contribution to our understanding of the Gospel. I have tried to show that when we abandon the mistaken idea that this treatment is essentially a mechanical process of bringing together isolated "proof-texts" and their supposed "fulfilments," and recognize that the governing intention is to exploit whole contexts selected as the varying expression of certain fundamental and permanent elements in the biblical revelation, we find genuine illumination upon theological questions of the first importance. There are places where the valuation of interpretations offered or presumed is a delicate problem. Each case is to be considered on its merits. In a broad way I would suggest that in any given case the question should be asked whether the meaning which the New Testament writer found in a passage of the Old Testament when he reflected on it in view of the gospel facts is an organic outgrowth or ripening of the original thought, or whether it amounts to no more than an arbitrary reading into a passage of a meaning essentially foreign to it. In the former case the theological value of the citation is likely to be greater. In the examples I have just given, Ps. ii, viii and cx, I believe reflection will show that the development of meaning is a living growth within the given environment, and that the doctrines associated with these passages by New Testament writers gain in depth and significance when we have regard to the original, historical intention of the psalms they cite. Without pursuing this problem further, I would submit that, while there is a fringe of questionable, arbitrary or even fanciful exegesis, the main line of interpretation of the Old Testament exemplified in the New is not only consistent and intelligent in itself, but also founded upon a genuinely historical understanding of the process of the religious— I should prefer to say the prophetic—history of Israel as a whole.

In conclusion, I would offer some corollaries regarding the character of New Testament theology, as a model of Christian theology in general. In the recent past an impatient reaction against the speculative systems of earlier periods took the form of attempts to ground

K

Christian theology upon "religious experience," conceived to be immune from the assaults of philosophical scepticism and historical criticism alike. That movement has now spent itself, and it is not necessary to rehearse either its achievements or its weaknesses. But it may be useful to recall, for the sake of contrast, the way in which it dealt with the biblical material. It set out to show that the genesis of New Testament theology could be accounted for out of the "religious experience" of the primitive Christians. That the evidence available for reconstructing that experience was scanty had to be admitted. But in the Pauline epistles there seemed to be a good deal of information about the inner life of one at least of the creators of Christian theology. Sustained attempts were made to show that Paul's theology was spun out of his experience of conversion on the Damascus road, and the "visions and revelations of the Lord" which ensued, whether these were conceived as "mystical" or as "prophetic" in character. But such attempts were doomed to failure. Paul refuses to exploit his "visions and revelations of the Lord" as a basis for doctrine. He alludes to them reluctantly, and only because his *bona fides* as a Christian teacher and prophet had been impugned. The ἄρρητα ῥήματα (II Cor. xii. 4) which he heard in paradise remain unspoken. *That* he heard such words the Corinthians should know, in order that they may rightly estimate both his qualifications and his limitations; *what* he heard is no concern of theirs. His "religious experience" is a private affair. He would speak of it only "to himself and to God" (I Cor. xiv. 28). Nor does he ever make his conversion experience the basis for doctrine, though he alludes to it obliquely, from time to time, in explication or corroboration of his teaching. It is of course true that any theology speedily becomes abstract and barren which does not verify itself in experience; Paul's did so verify itself. But this is a different matter from making such experience its ground, and this Paul never did. He expressly bases his theology upon the *kerygma* as illuminated by the prophecies of the Old Testament; or, in other words, upon the historical facts which he had "received" (ὃ καὶ παρέλαβον) from competent witnesses, set in the larger historical framework witnessed, both as fact and as meaning, by the prophetic writers. Upon this fundamental material he sets reason and imagination to work, in the context of an active Christian life of labour, prayer and charity within the *koinonia* of the Church, and so brings forth his massive theology for the enlightenment and guidance of generations of Christian believers.

If even Paul, who does in his letters so "unlock his heart," found a securer basis than his own "experience" for the theology he taught, still more is this true of other New Testament writers, whose experience in any case has to be conjectured, since they say nothing about it. This was not what early Christian preachers talked about. On the day of Pentecost, we are informed, their theme was not the amazing experience of being possessed by the Holy Spirit: it was "the mighty works of God" (τὰ μεγαλεῖα τοῦ θεοῦ, Acts ii. 11). Similarly, in the First Epistle of Peter, those whom God has "called out of darkness into his marvellous light" do not talk about the experience of enlightenment, but about "the victorious achievements" (ἀρεταί) of God (I Pet. ii. 9). And these mighty works, these ἀρεταί, are known through the testimony to the *Heilstatsachen*, the "saving facts" of the Gospel, understood in their total context.

If however in some quarters New Testament theology has been explained as nothing but the rationalizing of Christian "experience," others have laid stress upon a speculative element in it, akin to Hellenistic thought of the period, and have sometimes gone so far as to represent it as little more than a special case of the general development of popular religious ideas in the Hellenistic world. It is certainly true that the development of Christian theology was profoundly influenced by the religious thought of Hellenism, and it cannot be questioned that this influence is already at work in the New Testament, notably in some parts of the Pauline epistles, in the Epistle to the Hebrews, and in the Fourth Gospel. I see no reason to regret this, or to make any such attempts to minimize it as are often made at the present time. In the providence of God it was the Greeks who taught mankind the use of the logical faculty, and the early Church profited greatly by being their pupil. Eusebius and other Fathers were not mistaken in believing that the Greeks had provided a *praeparatio evangelica*. Origen, Augustine, Thomas Aquinas and many others did good and lasting service to the understanding of the Gospel by their acute use of the methods and categories of Greek philosophy. I am not among those who deplore their influence, nor am I persuaded by those who tell us that the great task of theologians of this generation is to purge Christian theology of the last dregs of Platonism.

All this, however, is matter of opinion. What is certain is that while the theology of the New Testament contains a substantial Hellenistic element, its fundamental structure, on the other hand, is not Hellenistic but biblical; and this biblical substructure is so firmly bonded into the whole edifice that no amount of Hellenizing ever destroyed, or ever could destroy, its basic character. In the controversy with Gnosticism in the second and third centuries the main point at issue was whether the Christian faith could be detached from its biblical and historical basis and presented as a form of Hellenistic theosophy. Victory in the controversy lay decisively with the party which rejected the Gnostic proposals for a thorough Hellenizing of Christianity, though this party included theologians who made extensive use of Greek philosophical categories to formulate and defend Christian dogma. During the period when the Greek spirit was most active in shaping the dogmatic system, creed and liturgy continued to bear witness to the biblical foundation. The ecumenical creed of Christendom as it emerged from the period of stress in the form called (with doubtful propriety) Nicene confesses Christ who "rose again according to the Scriptures," and the Holy Spirit "who spoke by the prophets." It thereby ties the whole Christian faith to its biblical origins. The two evangelical sacraments are directly based upon biblical foundations, whatever importance Hellenistic ideas may have had in elucidating and extending their significance. Baptism is the expression of that central conception which we have seen to be most deeply rooted in the scheme of *testimonia*, the conception of death and resurrection through which the Church came into being and through which each several member is incorporate in the Son of Man, and a branch of the true Vine. The Eucharist rehearses the passion and resurrection of Christ in terms of the covenant-sacrifice and sin-offering of the Servant of the Lord, who is also the Son of Man. Early liturgies repeat and emphasize the primitive insistence on the creative and redeeming acts of God to which the Old Testament bears witness, as the antecedents of His final act of re-creation and redemption in Christ. The very ancient series of lections for the season of Advent, for example, still preserved in the Roman rite, includes the great prophecies of Isaiah which we have noted as part of the primitive substructure: the vision of glory in chapter vi, the prophecy of Immanuel in chapter vii, the Stem of Jesse in chapter xi, the foundation-stone of Zion in chapter xxviii, the ordination of the Servant in chapter xlii. These are examples of the way in which the ancient body of scriptural testimonies was incorporated in the forms of the Church's worship, which thus conserved intact the biblical and historical foundations of Christian theology while the subtle processes of Hellenistic philosophy elaborated the superstructure.

The work that the Hellenistic theologians did was an example to theologians of every period. They sought an expression for the fundamental truths of the Gospel in terms which would give them relevance to the large questions which in that age were being asked about God, man and the universe. We in turn have the task of giving them relevance to the large questions which are being asked by men of our time. But if theology seeks an accommodation with temporary fashions of thought by cutting loose from its firm foundations in *kerygma* and testimonies, as it has sometimes done, it declines into insignificance, and has in fact nothing to say to the world which the world may not learn elsewhere. The challenge of a new period with its peculiar problems should force us back to the pit from whence we were digged and the rock from whence we were hewn.

INDEX OF BIBLICAL REFERENCES

1. *Old Testament and Apocrypha*

139

Printed in Great Britain by
The Camelot Press Ltd., London and Southampton